Contents

e

Editorial
BRIAN WARD

Terry Eagleton recently described Beckett's work as an extended attempt to 'eff the ineffable'. Beckett is exemplary in that, after a long period of gestation, he developed a language and an approach that could be manipulated for confident forays into various different media - theatre, film, radio, novels and poetry. If each medium is seen as a site, each foray was highly site-specific and indeed, made the site itself very apparent.

This *building material* examines the process of gestation in architecture, favouring the private works of the architect over those which become the object of public scrutiny and consumption. It concentrates on the generative rather than the descriptive. Using the architects' notebook as a receptacle of observations and proposals, investigations and dreams, it presents a glimpse of how architects record and process the world.

Meanwhile, the articles address the use of this work as a foundation for architectural assaults on Eagleton's 'ineffable', suggesting that with the continual emergence of new media, there might be an argument for considering (or even designing) the design process itself. A deliberately chosen (but open) strategy might suggest particular tools rather than allowing the tools themselves to dictate how the work develops. Accordingly, the opportunities and limitations of various media in common usage are also addressed.

Architects are almost unique within the visual arts in that they rarely get to work directly on the artefact that is the fruit of their labour, relying instead on what have been called 'intervening media'. It would seem prudent that consideration is given to the choice and use of these media in the private works with which architects record the existing world and formulate approaches to amend it.

Myself and the editorial committee wish to record our appreciation to all those who contributed selections from their notebooks. We are mindful that of all architectural documents it is perhaps the most private. We would also like to extend special thanks to John Grade and Wendy Judge

Paulo Mendes da Rocha: "Where is the giraffe in my project"
MIRIAM DUNN

The following is the first of a two-part interview with Paulo Mendes da Rocha in his office in the centre of Sao Paulo on a hot winter's day. In an office full of objects - eroded stones, a canvas chair etc - there is a chalkboard full of ideas, the centre of his universe. He is open and honest in his delivery of ideas, his words being carefully chosen and not premeditated. A relaxed dialogue ensues in which we explore how architecture might provoke an interaction with the environment around us, thereby creating a stimulus for our existence.

Your work engages with the land in a very deliberate manner. How do you regard the land of the Americas in particular? And to what extent do you see the land in general as part of architecture?
The presence of nature is very strong in Brazil. It informs the collective imagination from which one then chooses particular aspects of interest. It is like a universal consciousness which guides us all. It is also the basis for an interesting conversation about the type of experience that Nature can enable. This is relevant, of course, not only to Brazilian Architecture, but also to the whole world.

For instance, the quite recent spectacle of the so-called 'Discovery of America', can be seen in the same light as today's exploration of space, ie. as an expression of human endeavour. An immense amount of courage was required to navigate those unknown seas, but the physical action was inspired by both imagination and scientific speculation - the speculation acting as the substratum of the expeditions. The relationship between Galileo and Columbus is an important one - theories were formulated and then the adventure of discovery was undertaken as their confirmation. We must remember that the 'Discovery of America' is a most recent phenomenon, only 500 years old, and we Brazilians are a product of it. That spirit of discovery is still alive in Brazil.

How do you think that this impacts on its architecture?
Staying on the subject of Science and Technology, we come to an issue that is fundamental to Architecture, which is that it is a human activity that involves all of knowledge's disciplines — Philosophy, Art and Technology (ie. wish and possibility) - all at the same time. And as it's impossible for an Architect to know about everything, we then have to know about everything in a very particular way ie. through architecture. Architecture is a particular body of knowledge — it is one of the most extraordinary expressions of Man's

existence on this planet: it makes nature habitable and in doing so, it builds the world's habitat. We are fortunate in South America in that we get to witness a very vivid expression of that phenomenon.

But it is a universal consciousness, and today more than ever, the formation of such a consciousness must involve a conception of nature as a state of flux, as a passage, as a transformation. This can be seen in the ecological movement which argues for man's involvement in nature as an intelligent agent. Architecture nowadays should therefore be taught as an expression of Man's transformation of nature, albeit one distorted by political, sociological and cultural circumstances.

How does man — or an architect - apply himself in transforming nature?
I am interested in literature on the slow passage from the Middle Ages to the Renaissance, for instance Erwin Panofsky's beautiful writings about the struggle to form the humanist consciousness. Today I see contained within ecological discourse the notion of the emergence of a new popular culture. We are at a moment of transformation which by necessity is one of great contradiction and pain, similar to the cultural shift from the Middle Ages into the Renaissance. But I believe in the coming of this new popular consciousness.

You have spoken previously about the notion of the 'city for all'. Is it possible to draw this idea of a city? Or can it only occur through evolution?
This is a weakness of architects. They think things have to be drawn and designed in a definitive way and therefore we have never succeeded in creating the 'city for all'. The city is still a place of great conflict and class divisions. One must distance oneself from the notion of an ideal city, it cannot exist for it is purely a human ideal. The real city will never be concluded. But although we cannot possibly design an ideal city, we can easily imagine our work as exemplary actions. (Exemplary, that is, as distinct from examples). I see the Baia de Vitorio project, for instance, as an exemplary project, in that it transforms nature in a stimulating way.

Do you see this in the way the forms engage with the land?
We are not talking about Nature as an object of contemplation. We're not talking about landscape. I mean the phenomenology of nature! Fluid mechanics, solid mechanics, the force of gravity, plumbness, the weight of stones, geometry... It's not a design to be

observed simply as a form, but as a transformation that produces stimulating results, a new image of the city. Fundamentally, it is the success of technology. But it should not be considered purely from a technical point of view. A poet who trusts the workings of his language does not become a mere mechanic of words. I know that I can speak poetically and lyrically within the restricted means of that language, as long as I am moved by something.

What moves you is desire! We have to build this desire! Desire is the fundamental attribute of life in that it generates activity. And activity ultimately makes sense of our life. It is the only hope we have of being effectively stimulating. Desire generates language and is hence the crucial stimulus.

And what is the result of this desire?

There is a beautiful analysis of Piero di Cosimo's 'Vulcan and Aeolus' by Panofsky which every architect should read. It is a large painting full of Mediaeval and Renaissance iconography and iconology. Two old men are depicted talking by a fire in the foreground, while the background includes, amongst other things, the structural members of a hut under construction, a donkey at work and a giraffe! Panofsky describing the scene, notes that one of the old men is a cripple, his leg being in a funny position. He infers that he is Vulcan, the god of Fire, who was expelled from the pantheon for misbehaving and hurt his leg in the fall. The other man, is Aeolus, the god of Wind. Wind and fire together create a forge, enabling the manufacture of a horseshoe. Wearing a horseshoe the donkey can work for them - it is transformed into a machine! This, of course, is the story of technology. But what about the wonderful Giraffe? What is its part in the painting? Panofsky tells us that it is there because the Caliph of Baghdad had sent the Pope a giraffe as a present and that Di Cosimo, attempting to depict knowledge, felt compelled to represent the links between the East and West.

It must be remembered that the painting is a work of the imagination — nobody posed for it. But Panofsky is able to reveal the ideas embodied in it. We are back to the concept of a substratum, which should be fundamental to an Architect's endeavours. We are not concerned with making architecture. We are concerned with trying to solve crucial problems of our existence. Only in attempting this will the monumental dimension of beauty appear. Today, architecture cannot rely on the production of metaphors and symbols. There are no more churches, palaces or monuments. Architecture must instead attempt to embody the wishes and necessities of contemporary society. It must inspire a discourse such as Panofsky's. His text should therefore be a bible for every Architect: What are you saying when you do this with your building? And this? If paintings can contain a discourse, then surely it is fitting to ask: 'what discourse is contained in works of architecture?' You look at a building and what does it say? Only if it speaks can desire be stimulated into discourse.

You must look at your architecture and ask where is Vulcan? Where is Aeolus? And where is the giraffe in my project? I think about Architecture like this, in this delirium. But I am the master of my imagination! Not a victim.

This interview was recorded on DVD in Sao Paulo, 26th August 2005. Supported by the Arts Council. Translation by Marta Moriera (São Paulo), Tiago Faria and Nelson Faustino Carvalho, (Dublin).

Paulo Mendes da Rocha belongs to the last generation of Modernist architects. Born in Vitoria, 1928, and educated in São Paulo, he is one of the key architects in the so-called 'Paulista School' centered in São Paulo. He is Professor at the Faculty of Architecture, São Paulo. His work is preoccupied with the monumentality of structure combined with a weightless quality, exemplified by such projects as the Contemporary Sculpture Museum of São Paulo, MuBE and the Chapel of São Pedro. In 2006, Paulo Mendes da Rocha was awarded the Pritzker Prize for Architecture.

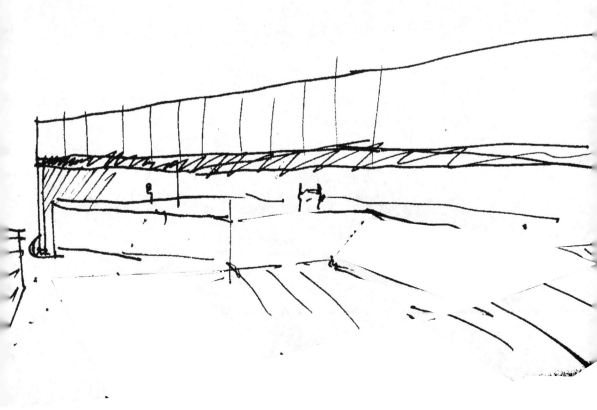

3

```
Command: rec
RECTANG
Specify first corner point or [Chamfer/Elevation/Fillet/Thickness/Width]:
Specify other corner point or [Dimensions]: @1800,900
Command: rec
RECTANG
Specify first corner point or [Chamfer/Elevation/Fillet/Thickness/Width]:
Specify other corner point or [Dimensions]: @500,320
Command: i
INSERT
Specify insertion point or [Scale/X/Y/Z/Rotate/PScale/PX/PY/PZ/PRotate]:
Specify rotation angle <0.00>: 90
Command: i
INSERT
Specify insertion point or [Scale/X/Y/Z/Rotate/PScale/PX/PY/PZ/PRotate]:
Specify rotation angle <0.00>:
Command:
Command: m
MOVE 1 found
Specify base point or displacement: Specify second point of displacement or
<use first point as displacement>:
Command: l
LINE Specify first point: <Osnap off>
Specify next point or [Undo]:
Specify next point or [Undo]: *Cancel*
Command: o
OFFSET
Specify offset distance or [Through] <Through>: 10
Select object to offset or <exit>:
Specify point on side to offset:
Command: l
LINE Specify first point:
Specify next point or [Undo]:
Specify next point or [Close/Undo]:
Command: tr
TRIM
Current settings: Projection=UCS, Edge=Extend
Select cutting edges ...
Select objects: 1 found
Command: tr
TRIM
Current settings: Projection=UCS, Edge=Extend
Select cutting edges ...
Select objects: 1 found
Command: tr
TRIM
Current settings: Projection=UCS, Edge=Extend
Select cutting edges ...
Select objects: 1 found
Select objects:
Select object to trim or shift-select to extend or [Project/Edge/Undo]:
INTELLIZOOM
Command: _explode 1 found
Command: tr
TRIM
Current settings: Projection=UCS, Edge=Extend
Select cutting edges ...
Select objects: 1 found
Select object to trim or shift-select to extend or [Project/Edge/Undo]:
Command:
** STRETCH **
Specify stretch point or [Base point/Copy/Undo/eXit]: <Ortho on>
Command:
** STRETCH **
Specify stretch point or [Base point/Copy/Undo/eXit]:
Command: tr
TRIM
Current settings: Projection=UCS, Edge=Extend
Select cutting edges ...
Select objects: 1 found
Select objects:
Select object to trim or shift-select to extend or [Project/Edge/Undo]:
Command:
TRIM
Current settings: Projection=UCS, Edge=Extend
Select cutting edges ...
Select objects: 1 found
Select object to trim or shift-select to extend or [Project/Edge/Undo]:
Command:
** STRETCH **
Specify stretch point or [Base point/Copy/Undo/eXit]:
Command:
** STRETCH **
Specify stretch point or [Base point/Copy/Undo/eXit]:
Command: tr
TRIM
Current settings: Projection=UCS, Edge=Extend
Select cutting edges ...
Select objects: 1 found
Select objects:
Select object to trim or shift-select to extend or [Project/Edge/Undo]:
Command: br
BREAK Select object:
Specify second break point or [First point]:
Point or option keyword required.
Specify second break point or [First point]:
Command:
BREAK Select object:
Specify second break point or [First point]:
Command: tr
TRIM
Current settings: Projection=UCS, Edge=Extend
Select cutting edges ...
Select objects: 1 found
Select objects:
Select object to trim or shift-select to extend or [Project/Edge/Undo]:
Command:
TRIM
Current settings: Projection=UCS, Edge=Extend
Select cutting edges ...
Select objects: 1 found
Select objects:
Select object to trim or shift-select to extend or [Project/Edge/Undo]:
Command: co
COPY 1 found
Specify base point or displacement:  <Osnap on> Specify second point of
displacement or <use first point as displacement>:
Command: tr
TRIM
Current settings: Projection=UCS, Edge=Extend
Select cutting edges ...
Select objects: 1 found
```

Orla Murphy and Elaine Naughton live and work in the BMW region.

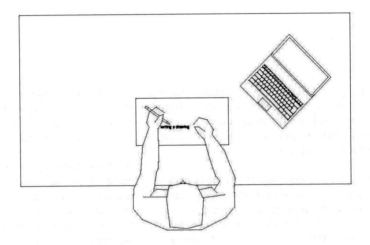

Writing a drawing……..

4

The trouble with drawing
MARK PRICE

It could take years to dash off a quick sketch. Not the sketch itself of course, but finding a way to begin[i]. "How am I to draw when it's all been done before, so much better? What should I include? How can I hope to capture what I see on paper?"[ii]

At the centre of this conundrum of drawing lie both the potential and the limits of the human body in three-dimensional space. Drawing takes trouble and time, it entails alchemic operations between dimensions, invoking the transformative power of *mimesis*.[iii] Drawing by hand opposes the productive tendencies of modern life, by insisting on gesture as the basis of representation.

Architects are in two minds about sketching: the sketch can be something useful in working out designs, but otherwise it belongs to the years of study and trips, before the years of practice. Sketching when not working out a specific design problem is what you did when you were learning, before you started *doing*. Instrumental thinking is deeply ingrained in architectural practice. Architects rarely doubt that what is useful for them in producing their designs is also good for architecture.

In fact, as Dalibor Vesley asserts, there is 'a gap between the domain of situated knowledge and that of productive knowledge. This gap, which represents a radical discontinuity with the natural world, reduces the cognitive value of productive knowledge and makes it merely a technical tool.' [iv]

This gap can be bridged by sketching *en plein air*. The trouble is finding the time.

Musee imaginaire
From at least the time of Villard de Honnecourt, travel sketches have served as a source of formal ideas and references for architects 'back in the office', regardless of whether or not these sketches were made by the architect himself. Herman Hertzberger gives his collection of sketchbooks the title *musee imaginaire*.[v]

When an architect puts his or her idea on paper, the result acts as a sort of new 'fact on the ground', which in turn becomes a source of information for – and thereby an influence on – the idea. The putting down on paper is what transforms the work. The relationship between the idea and the drawing is therefore not one in which the drawing represents the idea: the drawing in fact becomes the idea, and this idea may spawn others. In the words of John Berger:

It is the actual drawing that forces the artist to look at the object in front of him, to dissect it in his mind's eye and put it together again... A line, an area of tone, is not really important because it records what you have seen, but because of what it will lead you on to see[vi].

The architect must think at a certain scale, because not all information is useful at all times. The *beaux arts* idea of *parti* acknowledges the essential reductiveness of design. Perhaps 'selectiveness' might serve our description better: through selection of visual data, the architect asserts control. By transforming visual information into manual activity, into a gesture, the process of remaking the world begins. By having to draw, through the difficulty of rendering the constituent parts in a satisfactory relationship, the artist or architect finds the correct - which is to say natural - order of the world, including the natural and built realms.

Drawing initiates the process of transformation from concept to three dimensions. The drawing on paper may be a two-dimensional thing, but only if it is considered purely as an instruction. In all its material aspects, including the performative, the drawing exists already in three dimensions.

Stranger than fiction

In painting, until well into the twentieth century, the subject was always... taken from nature...[it] is held to exist prior to its representation. This is not true of architecture, which is brought into existence through drawing... Drawing in architecture is not done after nature, but prior to construction; it is not so much produced by reflection on the reality outside the drawing, as productive of a reality that will end up outside the drawing.[vii]

Insofar as architectural drawings contain projected realities they are imaginary, and so are like fictions. But architectural drawing frequently hovers in an ambiguous space between imaginative and measurable reality.[viii] In an age of scepticism with regard to everything except science and technology, Umberto Eco makes the case for other types of truth:

As far as the world is concerned, we find that the laws of universal gravitation are those established by Newton, or that it is true that Napoleon died on Saint Helena on 5 May 1821. And yet, if we keep an open mind, we will always be prepared to revise our convictions the day science formulates the great laws of the cosmos differently, or a historian discovers unpublished documents proving that Napoleon died on a Bonapartist ship as he attempted to escape. On the other hand, as far as the world of books is concerned, propositions like 'Sherlock Holmes was a bachelor', 'Little Red Riding-Hood is eaten by the wolf and then freed by the woodcutter', or 'Anna Karenina commits suicide' will remain true for eternity, and no one will ever be able to refute them.[ix]

As far as the world of buildings is concerned, a building might be true if it exists, but a building or architectural drawing could still claim to be true if it corresponds with something 'inside our head'.[x] The truth of architectural drawings could be said to depend on the extent to which they imaginatively recreate the world:

Every act of drawing was, for Leonardo, an act of looking and analysis, and it was on the basis of these analyses that the human creator can remake the world. Thus the flying machine and the 'Mona Lisa' comparably remake the natural world on nature's own terms, fully obedient to natural causes and effects. One is an artificial 'bird'; the other is an artificial remaking of the visual experience of another's physical presence.[xi]

Hubris

The drawing has intrinsic limitations of reference. Not all things architectural... can be arrived at through drawing. There must also be a penumbra of qualities that might only be seen darkly and with great difficulty through it...[xii] Robin Evans

There are reasons to suspect that contemporary developments will go a long way towards airbrushing out these shadowy forms, and that this will impoverish architectural culture. This 'penumbra' of qualities may not be something available at the click of a mouse. It could be that these dimensions may not be willed into architecture, that they only result from non-productive activity.[xiii]

As everyone knows, computers become increasingly useful as the scale of work and repetition increases. This efficiency of scale promotes a narrowly instrumental view of drawing. Drawings take time (even sketches, as we have noted) and computer-generated drawings also take time. But the technology allows drawings or parts of drawings to be copied easily and reassembled quickly. This facility encourages design by collage, and by repetition.

Computer drawings are as intrinsically limited in their ability to represent space as any other type of drawings. But computers foster a certain set of illusions with regard to spatial representation: that there is somehow a model of the project (or even a 'real building') inside the computer; that every operation is taking place at full scale (when in fact there is no scale until either a representation is selected or the building is made); that the most difficult and significant decisions ('which scale' and 'which point of view' to select at any time) are no longer difficult and therefore not significant; and that perspective projections generated by the computer, either in rapid series or not, somehow constitute '3D'. These effects are willed into being by the central promise of convenience: designing things, like housework, can be made easier using gadgets. In addition, the computational power available lends itself to elaborate surface rendering, and this tendency coincides with an architectural 'culture of skin'. The line drawings of modernism on the other hand, relied on radical operations in volume, using minimal surface detail. Much more was being claimed by showing less.

We have used mathematics and machines to create a model of perfection to represent the space-time continuum, but we have all the while been held in check by knowledge of our corporeal limits. This knowledge begins to be acquired by the newborn infant, and it allows us to maintain the hope that – were it not for these physical limits – we could completely represent and therefore control reality. The emergence of cyberspace as a design tool has removed that knowledge but not the underlying condition of being in the world, and thereby left us disoriented. Slavoj Zizek explains this in another context:

So the only consistent answer to the question 'Why does the superfluous prohibition emerge, which merely prohibits the impossible?' is: in order to obfuscate this inherent impossibility - that is, in order to sustain the illusion that, were it not for the externally imposed prohibition, the full ('incestuous') gratification would be possible. Far from acting as the 'repressive agency preventing us from gaining access to the ultimate object of desire', the function of the paternal figure is thus quite the opposite, to relieve us of the debilitating deadlock of desire, to 'maintain hope'...

The problem with 'Oedipus on-line' is thus that what is missing in it is precisely this 'pacifying' function of the paternal figure which enables us to obfuscate the debilitating deadlock of desire – hence the strange mixture of 'everything is possible' (since there is no positive prohibiting figure) and an all-pervasive frustration and deadlock that characterizes the subject's experience of cyberspace.[xiv]

Moore's Law[xv] promises an almost infinite increase in information capacity, and together with accelerated computational power, the future is imagined as a time when the designer will be 'freed up' to do whatever he or she wants. The problem with this scenario is the implied relationship between a designer, her ideas and the drawing: with sufficiently efficient production of drawings, anything will be possible. In this imagined future, the trouble with drawing can be abolished, and ideas can come out much more quickly, so we can get more of our ideas out. Or simply, more efficient production of drawings = more efficient production of ideas.

The equation collapses when we consider that it was the difficulty of drawing that served in the first instance to both engender creative participation, and to mask the impossibility of direct representation. Ideas are no more amenable to exhaustive description than space is: both elude any attempt at a complete visual account. The impossibility of complete representation is a sort of wisdom for architects, because it is in fact the way the world is. Technology, which promised to remove the difficulty of drawing to scale, fails to do so, yet insists on its emancipatory potential. The result is that the designer thinks 'now I can do anything', and is puzzled to discover that, in fact, there never was any chance he could 'do anything'.

The claims of technology to the problems of representing space have extended beyond matters of efficiency and production. It is claimed that computer drawing programmes are not just more efficient but more authentic. The promotional literature conflates '3D' with 'representation of 3D', so that computer-generated perspective becomes identified with three-dimensional space itself.

The history of means of representation is seen from this point of view as a series of technological advances. The conventionality and unreliability of perspective projection has been described in detail by others such as Ernst Gombrich and Nelson Goodman ('Briefly, the behaviour of light sanctions neither our usual nor any other way of rendering space; and perspective provides no absolute or independent standard of fidelity.'[xvi]) Computer-animated 'walk-throughs' are created using perspective projections arranged in series. The claim for the authenticity of the CAD image results from this confusion concerning spatial representation, coupled with a historically accelerating impatience with the speed of development of the means of production, extended to the field of design. This has been further underscored by contemporary certainties about technical instrumentalism.

What emerges is what Vesley calls the 'grey zone':

The arbitrary nature of the relation between the sphere of experience and the sphere of concepts or ideas is the main characteristic of the grey zone. It is the source of unprecedented freedom to produce new works but also of an overwhelming relativism, loss of meaning, and narrowing range of cultural references – and, as a result, of a general cultural malaise.[xvii]

The very fact of 'emancipated representation' (that is, freed from the complicated entanglements between the world and the means of representing it) creates an autonomous representation from which information about the world is intentionally excluded. The designer is delivered from the world where design occurs in a dialogue between imagined reality and its representations, to one where the designer and the disembodied 'idea' are locked together in a closed, airless room. Apart from more general cultural concerns, this could presage an architecture which is more malleable in the interests of power.[xviii] This can be located generally in the process of (frequently violent) suppression of that which 'stands in the way of progress'.[xix] What stands in the way of progress is usually inconvenient, useless or troublesome information.

To the inhabitants of cyberspace, unperturbed by 'ineluctable modalities' of any sort, temporarily oblivious to creeping ageing-sickness-and-death (the ultimate point, surely, of cyberspace, the reason for that which Yves Lyon calls its 'negation of time and space'); for these people the world inside the counting machine might constitute a sustainable illusion. But a building will out eventually. Its spaces will manifest as spaces, things into which you can bump if you're not careful.

Architects, therefore, ought to take the trouble to draw, and not just as they are working out their 'ideas'. As discussed, their ideas may not properly be said to exist prior to their being drawn. So also their understanding of the problems for which they seek a solution may be dangerously incomplete. Le Corbusier sketched Istanbul, all the while worrying about the state of modern architecture (and what he was planning to do about it). Despite attempts to trace the provenance of important designs in a direct line to these sketch studies, maybe the importance does not lie in what the architect is sketching, as long as what he or she is doing is looking at the world. This information, however it *is* selected, just as long as it *is* selected, constitutes the best hope of an antidote to the 'grey zone'.

Sketches from nature or culture constitute a source of visual nourishment for architecture. The sketchbook (Hertzberger's musee imaginaire) acts as the 'space of communication' between this information and the working drawings of the architect. The point is that such information about the world, having been drawn by hand, is imaginatively acquired by the designer, and as such can enter into dialogue with those other products of his imagination, his ideas.[xx]

Footnotes

i 'When I was a child I could draw like Raphael. I have spent the rest of my life trying to draw like a child' (Attributed to Picasso).

ii The moment before one begins to draw can be daunting. There is the awful finality of choice – you must decide to draw this, at this very moment, and not all the other things. There is the nagging suspicion that you have become an amateur watercolourist. And trying to recover innocence of vision can entail loss of confidence.

iii See 'The Mimetic Nature of Architecture' in Architecture in the age of Divided Representation by Dalibor Vesley (MIT, 2004), p.366

iv Vesley, op.cit., page 300.

v See Notations of Herman Hertzberger (NAi, 2005).

vi John Berger, Drawing, in Permanent Red, Essays in Seeing (London, 1960), quoted by John Olley, Drawing – The Language of Representation and Thought in Design, published in The Architect and the Drawing (RIAI Dublin, 1989).p.16

vii Translations from Drawing to Building by Robin Evans (AA Files,12, summer 1986).p.7

viii I'm grateful to Tom de Paor for drawing my attention to his experience of finding for the first time a project designed by him on an Ordnance Survey map (Ballincollig Visitors' Centre). At such a moment, an architect must experience a 'dimensional shift' – the migration of an idea into the realm of situated reality, the architectural 'poacher-turned-gamekeeper'. (Other architects who generously .gave time to help me with this piece were: Cormac Allen, Derek Tynan, Gary Lysaght, Jim Murphy and John Tuomey)

ix On Literature by Umberto Eco (Vintage, 2006).p.5

x 'We want to have ourselves translated into stone and plant, we want to go for a walk in ourselves when we wander in these halls and gardens'. (The Gay science by F.Nietzsche, Trans. Walter Kaufmann, Vintage, 1974. page 280.)

xi Leonardo by Martin Kemp (Oxford, 2004).p.5

xii Evans, op.cit.p.5

xiii 'You will write if you write without thinking of the result in terms of a result, but think of the writing in terms of discovery, which is to say that creation must take place between the pen and the paper' (Gertrude Stein, 1930).

xiv 'The Fantasy in Cyberspace' by Slavoj Zizek, in The Zizek Reader (Oxford, 1999).p.116

xv Attributed to Gordon... Moore, a co-founder of Intel in 1965. The most common formulation is 'the doubling of the number of transistors on integrated circuits every 18 months'.

xvi 'Reality Remade' in Languages of Art, by Nelson Goodman (Harvester, 1968).

xvii Vesley, op.cit., page 34.

xviii The instrumental attitude to representation involves an a priori ordering of reality into what is or isn't considered useful for a given task. This is the basis of scientific and mathematical experimental dialogue since the time of Galileo. The decision of what is useful can be made by anyone, but in the case of mathematical drawing systems it can easily be made 'above the head' of the individual designer.

xix 'The industrialized world has tried to approximate paradise in its suburbs, with luxe, calme, volupte, cul-de-sac, cable television and two-car garages, and it has produced a soft ennui that shades over into despair and a decay of the soul, suggesting that paradise is already a gulag'. Hope in the Dark, by Rebecca Solnit (Nation Books, 2004).p.115-116

xx 'The initial idea is transformed as it comes into contact with the realities of the site ('site' characterized as both 'way of life' and 'place')' (Alvaro Siza).

Mark Price is an architect in Dublin. He teaches in UCD and has trouble with computers.

Sections from agadir

saffron, sorghum, maize, turnip, potato, courgette
bulb, just planted, harvested in november (?)

aspen, walnut, willow(?), apple, almond

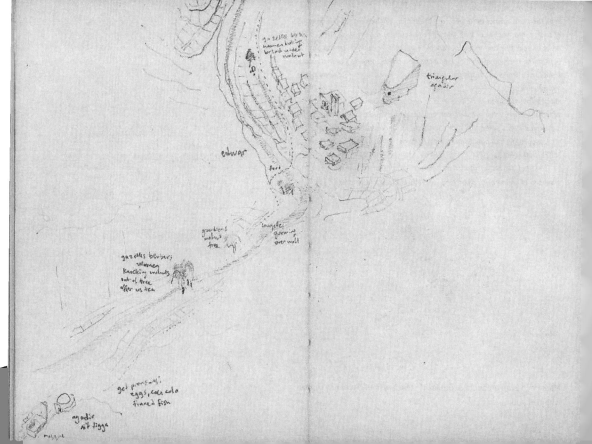

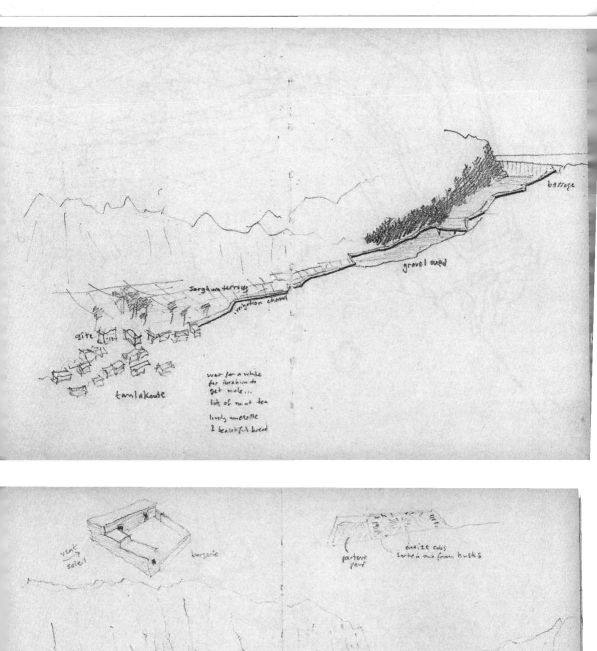

barrage

gravel oued

Sorghum terraces

irrigation channel

gite

tanlakoute

wait for a while
for Ibrahim to
get mule...
lots of mint tea

lively omelette
& beautiful bread

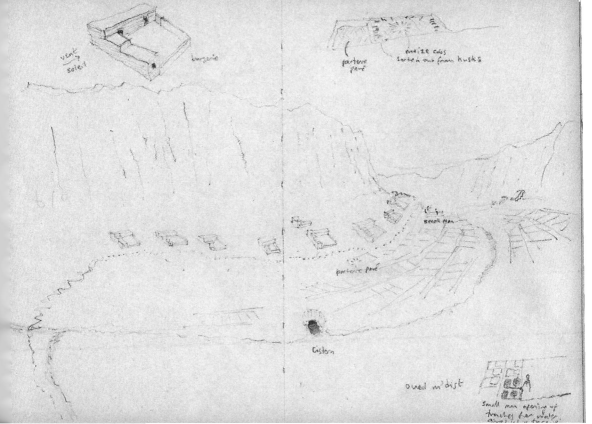

vent
soleil

bergerie

parterre
pavé

maize cobs
sorted out from husks

small man

parterre pavé

Cistern

oued m'dist

small man opening up
trenches for water

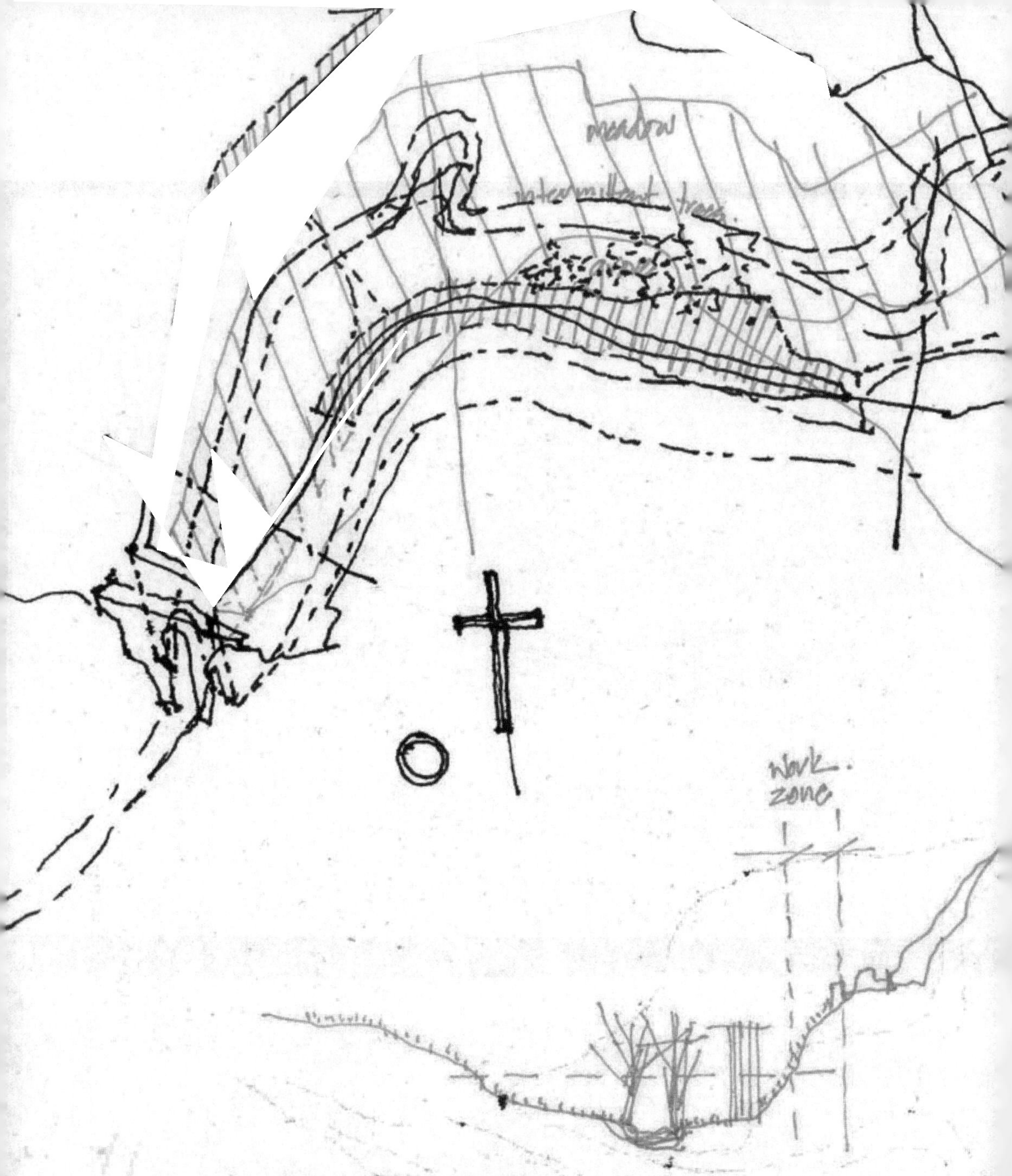

meadow

intermittent trees

work.
zone

definitely a wall scheme
not a stilt scheme tomas.
call 496 2614 for details.
ena.

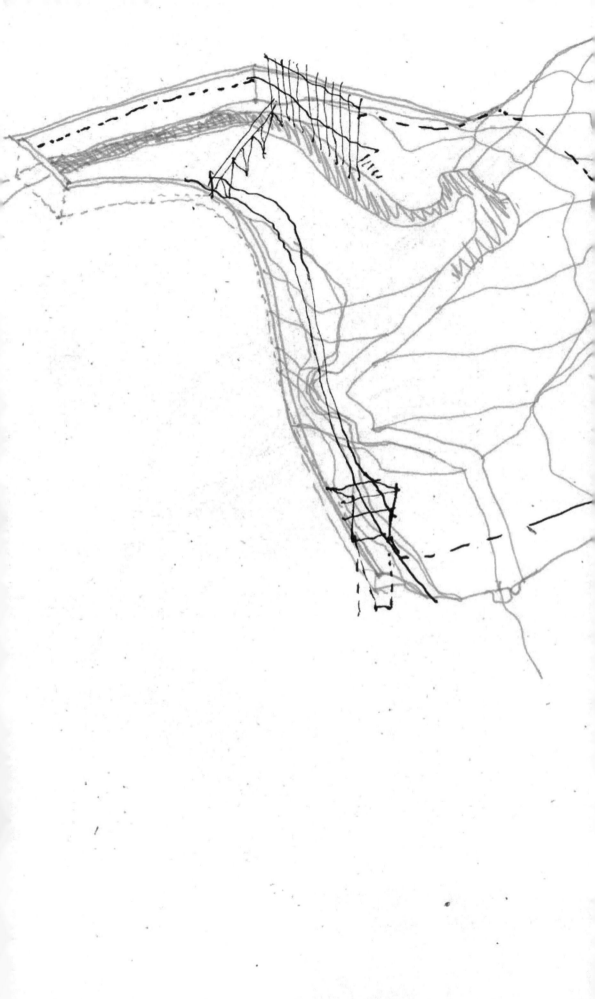

VALLUM – DEFENSIVE WALL OF EARTH OR STONE.
ANCIENT ROMANS CONSTRUCTED VALLUMS FROM
DIRT THROWN UP FROM A SURROUNDING FOSSE. – 'THE SUNKEN FOSSE OF HER SPINE'
WICKET WORK SYSTEM OF COAL MINING – 'BLOOD-HOLT'
NORTHERN WALES.

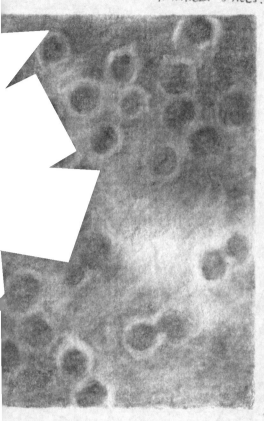

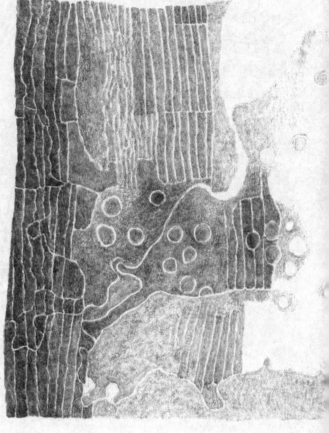

FEM.
(WHITE?)
BAN HUS? – NOT IN IRISH DICTIONARY
TO LOOK FROM BELOW THE BOG:
PORES. DARK WET BLACK. STATIC ROOTS.
WELLING, UNFOCUSED. SEAMS? CUTS?

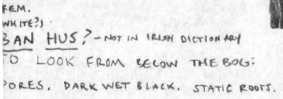

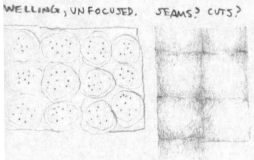

ORGAN VERTICALS TO THE EAST OF GIANT'S CAV
SIMILARLY TO VIEW FROM BELOW

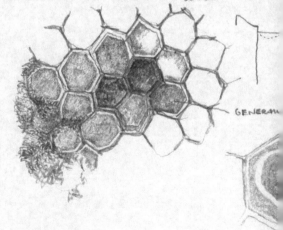

GENERAL

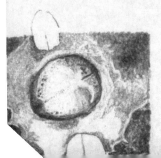

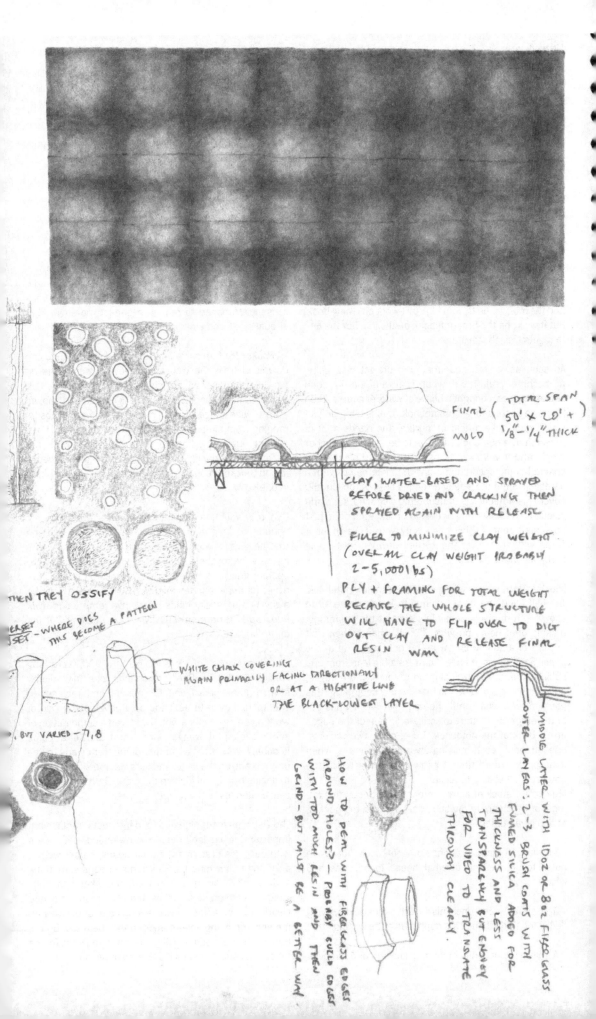

THEN THEY OSSIFY

...ERSET ...SET - WHERE DOES THIS BECOME A PATTERN

. BUT VARIED - 7,8

FINAL (TOTAL SPAN
MOLD   50' X 20' +)
        1/8" - 1/4" THICK

CLAY, WATER-BASED AND SPRAYED
BEFORE DRIED AND CRACKING THEN
SPRAYED AGAIN WITH RELEASE

FILLER TO MINIMIZE CLAY WEIGHT.
(OVERALL CLAY WEIGHT PROBABLY
2 - 5,000 lbs)

PLY + FRAMING FOR TOTAL WEIGHT
BECAUSE THE WHOLE STRUCTURE
WILL HAVE TO FLIP OVER TO DIG
OUT CLAY AND RELEASE FINAL
RESIN WALL

WHITE CHALK COVERING
AGAIN PRIMARILY FACING DIRECTIONALLY
OR AT A HIGHTIDE LINE
THE BLACK-LOWEST LAYER

HOW TO PEAL WITH FIBERGLASS EDGES
AROUND HOLES? - PROBABY BUILD EDGES
WITH TOO MUCH RESIN AND THEN
GRIND - BUT MUST BE A BETTER WAY

MIDDLE LAYER WITH 10oz or 8oz FIBERGLASS
OUTER LAYERS: 2-3 BRUSH COATS WITH
FUMED SILICA ADDED FOR
THICKNESS AND LESS
TRANSPARENCY BUT ENOUGH
FOR VIDEO TO TRANSLATE
THROUGH CLEARLY.

Notebooks are intrinsically useful things
DENNIS COTTER

I'm currently in the market for a new notebook. An electronic one this time, what we, the technically challenged public, insist on calling a laptop. I don't need it, and I'm not even that enthusiastic about it, but I need the promise of it, and the investment it will require, to find the motivation to actually start work on a new book. But it won't be the first notebook on the job, nor the one that gets the job started.

As soon as it was clear that this project was going to become real, I did what I always do in such circumstances. I bought a bottle of wine, of course. Then I went to Easons to get a notebook. This is a big project which could take a year of my life, and needs a lot of research. The notebook will have to be very portable but tough, and it will have to be aesthetically pleasing to ensure I enjoy spending time with it. I came out with a hardback about the size of a serious but not too lengthy novel. This notebook is undoubtedly a serious, scholarly colour. It has no writing or design of any kind on it, just its serious tone. I think I can work with it. So I took it home with the wine, and settled down to put some thoughts on paper.

I do this a lot. Every new project requires a new notebook. The half-filled one from last month is too cluttered to allow fresh thinking. Sensibly, I start at the beginning, making brief notes on which I can expand when I sit in front of a computer. I write on only one side of the paper. Sometimes, if I need to make a big leap from one subject to another, I will skip up to ten or more pages, and fold one page in half to mark a new beginning. This goes on for a while until one day I get a call while out of the office, and I start to scribble on one of the pages at the back of the notebook. That's okay, two projects, one notebook, each building towards the centre. When it happens a third time, I know in my heart that the notebook is heading for chaos.

My current stock of active notebooks includes this lot, most of which are in my shoulder bag, or in my pocket, at any given time:

- My diary. A diary is definitely a notebook. You leave notes to yourself about what needs to be done and when.

- The serious green one. This is still almost exclusively dedicated to the book I am supposed to be writing.

- A thinner blue one, randomly chosen and unloved really. It contains information on staff, potential staff, holiday requests, wage calculations and so on.

- Small paperback 100-page *Aisling – in a class of its own* with a pinkish cover, clearly a schoolkids thing. Found it at home when I took on a job updating recipes for a book re-issue. Managed to remain a one-job notebook, but should really come out of the bag now.

- *A Pocket Mod.* This is a fantastic gadget which you can download from the website pocketmod.com. It is an A4 sheet of paper which, with a few folds and one cut, becomes a tiny booklet of eight pages. You can choose from a wide range of design features on the website, ranging from simple lines to calendars to games. I use nothing but simple lines, of course. If you print it onto decent quality paper, the *Pocket Mod* will last for weeks in your pocket, replacing all the illegible scraps of paper in one go.

- In my wallet, a tiny notebook of a dozen pages, hand made by a good friend in New Zealand. Each one that he gives away has one important piece of useful information for the chosen recipient. Mine contains the opening line of a simple joke because I cannot remember a joke for more than ten minutes. He imagines this to be a debilitating social inadequacy. *Two jump leads walk into a bar. The barman says: "Now lads, don't be starting anything here".*

When we opened *Café Paradiso* back in 1993, everything was in notebooks. One for costings, one for building stuff, but a special one for menus and recipes. Or two, maybe even three. Early on, I developed a way of working on new dishes which involved a combination of sentences and drawings. Once a first draft of a recipe is done, I write it out a number of different ways to see how it reads on the page. And I draw some sketches of it to decide how it will look on the plate. Both of these can cause changes to the recipe.

The visual element of plated food in a restaurant is very important. It has long been acknowledged that we eat with our eyes first, and then our noses, before we put anything in our mouths. So if a dish needs something added, taken away or replaced, the sketches help. They are very crude sketches, but I can read them very clearly. In fact, any chef who spends a year or two with me ends up being able to understand them too. By the time someone is actually able to draw in my style for me to read, it usually means it's time to move on.

The sentence writing came about when I realised that the thing that people actually buy in a restaurant is a sentence on a menu. Mostly, the words are familiar enough to conjure up a known dish, or at least a known food cooked in a known way – grilled asparagus, for example. But a lot of the dishes in *Café Paradiso* are not instantly recognisable. So I spend a lot of time trying to make the sentence do two things: firstly, describe the dish as best it can; and, secondly, make it attractive. Sometimes it happens that fixing the sentence, i.e. swapping the name of one ingredient for another simultaneously improves the sentence and the food.

While in the early days all of this was done on endless pages of notebooks, now it is done at a computer. I type the words, change them, move them around, and sometimes write the same sentence out six times in six different ways. Meanwhile the sketching survives, and is done on the backs of old menu pages. I'd like to be able to say that I miss the old notebooks for this purpose, but I simply don't miss having to carry them around.

The last major project, which took up most of last year, was when we bought the building where *Café Paradiso* is and decided to convert the upstairs into three townhouse guest rooms and an office for the restaurant. We decided to do the design and planning ourselves, using some builders who had done good work for us in the past. There's not much too it, right? Who needs architects and engineers? For some reason, I used a thinner notebook for that. Maybe I thought it was a small job! Or maybe I thought this would be a one-project notebook. I used the front for schedules, lists of things to do and budget costing. From the back, it was plans for the layout, income projections and details of the rooms, done in pen without a ruler, but including details of built in furniture, bed location and so on. This was later transferred to measured graph paper, but a lot of the instructions to the builders were from the notebook sketches. Naturally, the middle of the book filled up with menus for someone's 40th birthday, recipes for magazines, ideas jotted down in other restaurants and so on. In the end, the book just about survived the building project. I love a well-used notebook.

Notebooks are intrinsically useful things. The only empty notebooks I own are a couple that I was given early in the life of *Café Paradiso*. Well-thought out gifts, beautifully handmade and coloured, and intended to inspire great things. I don't know what it was, perhaps they were too beautiful to use, or maybe I couldn't think of anything worthy of them. They remain empty, while I have gone through dozens of cheap stationery shop books. I think I need a notebook to be a blank space, not a suggesting or leading one.

Denis Cotter and his partner Bridget opened *Café Paradiso* in Cork in 1993. He is also a teacher and writer whose books, such as The *Cafe Paradiso* Cookbook and *Paradiso* Seasons, have won numerous international awards. His cooking focuses on seasonal eating and has a strong relationship with local vegetable and cheese producers.

...TO TOP OF... ...DEEP ENOUGH RIGHT UP TO THOSE. WAS ORIGIN
A VOLCANO.
COLLAPSED FOR
LAKE.

TUKTUK

DEEP PARAPAT

10 k

HOUSE AT STOP BUT NOT GREAT. ME +
LOOK AROUND. DECIDED TO CHECK OUT
ELSE STAYING THERE. GOT OURSELVES A
TRADITIONAL TYPE HUT FOR 5,000 RP = $1!

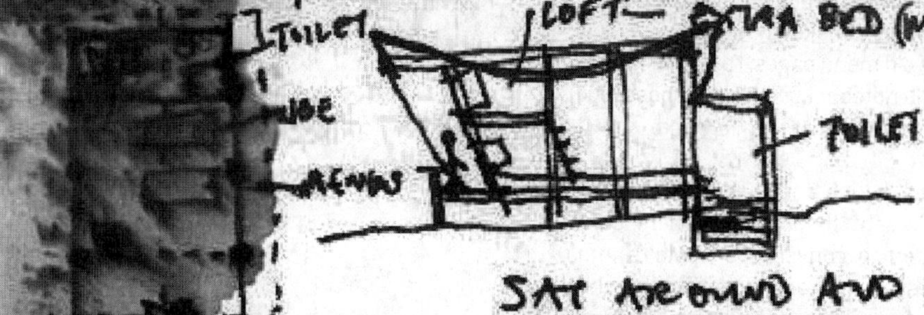

LOFT— EXTRA BED (ME)

TOILET

VIBE

MENUS

TOILET

STEPS

TERRACE   VIEW OF LAKE

VIEW TO
PARAPAT.

SAT AROUND AND VEGED. DID SOME
POSTCARDS. STARTED RAINING.
"GOVERNMENT RAIN." WENT TO
NEXT RESTAURANT AND HAD F...
DINNER + SING SONG.

SATURDAY 20TH SEPTEMBER

GOT UP ABOUT 10:00. SUN SHINY DAY. ME + AGNUS RENT...
BIKES. MINE 7,000 RP. CYCLED NORTH ALONG COAST TO STONE
CHAIRS OF VILLAGE ELDERS (KINGS) THEN TO SIMANINDO WH...
THEY HAVE A SMALL MUSEUM AT THE NORTHERN TIP O...
THE ISLAND. LOTS OF TRADITIONAL HOUSES ALONG THE WA...
LOTS OF KIDS & CHICKENS DOGS BUFFALO, DUCKS, CARTS + POTHOU...
RACED BACK. AGNUS WON ON A BETTER BIKE. SORE RE...
BOUGHT LITTLE WOODEN HOUSE SOUVENIR. 3,000 RP. THEN
DINNER AND EARLY TO BED.

SUNDAY 21ST SEPTEMBER (EQUINOX)

GOT UP AT 7:00 6:30 AND GOT BOAT TO PARAPAT. GOT 'BREAK...
FROM BUS COMPANY. THEN BUS TO BUKITTINGI. STOPPI...

N. 02° 40' 16.7"   WRITTEN ON   AT HOTSPRINGS, D...
                    — DUBB. IN   TEA AND TOILET
E. 98° 56' 14.1"   MAINSTREET   BUT ALREADY...
                    PARAPAT.   ASSAULTED BY...
OF T-SHIRTS SELLERS. FINALLY GOT TO BUKITTINGI AT ABOUT 11
SIMANLAN SAID THEY WERE FULL, WENT TO MURNI. OK

...UP AT 8:30. SHOWER AND BREAKFAST... CORE BUS A...

...RKFAST AT STAR CAFE. BUS TO JAKARTA 60,000 AC. SE...
...ARDS. 700 each. THEN MINIBUS TO BUS STATION. V...
...N AWAY STOPPING EVERY FEW YARDS TO PICK UP MORE...
...SENGERS GOING TO NEXT TOWN. RAILWAY LINE BESIDE
...L OPERATIONAL BUT DIDN'T SEE ANY LOCS. GOT TO PUT...
...ND WAITED MORE. FINALLY GOT OFF TOWARDS JAKARTA...
...OK LOOKS NICE LOTS OF TRADITIONAL HOUSES
...V LARGE BATS
...NG AROUND AT DUSK.
...Y BE FRUIT BATS!
...O EXPENSIVE DINNER.
...HED CRAP VIDEO.

...ESDAY 23rd SEPT.
...KE UP TO DESPERADOE'
...IDEO - HAS MOMENTS.
...V GET A LOT OF SLEEP. WHEN IT'S HILLY - BUS SHAKES + ROWS!
...ALLY GOT TO PORT BAKAHUNI FOR FERRY. STOPPING OFF
...KE OR TWICE AS USUAL. SAW ANOTHER PURE VIOLENCE VIDEO
...ST OF RAGE' - JAPANESE (?) DUBBED INTO MANDARIN WITH CHINESE
...ENGLISH SUBTITLES WITH INDONESIAN SUBTITLES SUPERIMPOSED! 
GOT ON BOAT 2HRS. TO
JAVA. (MERAK). QUITE
KNACKERED ALREADY.
HAZE GONE. VERY SUNNY.
HOT. ARRIVED ON JAVA.
MOTORWAY TO JAKARTA
LIKE A DIFFERENT COUNTRY
TRAFFIC, SKY SKRAPERS, IN

TYPICAL SOUTH
SUMATRA HOUSE
TILES
...ND —

...TS OF FACTORIES, SHOPPING CENTRES, ...KARTA. BUS DROPPED US OFF AT OFFICE. GOT TUK TUK 'BAJAJ'
...MELZE TO JALAN JAKSA. ME + JOE CHECKED PLACES OUT.
...MND 'JUSNA' HOSTEL END OF ALLEYWAY. OCEAN BOY
...AMPED. WE WE IN ONE ROOM AFANGS IN ANOTHER CUPBOARD
...000 RP. × AFANGS 9,000 RP. HAD A DRINK. THEN SLEPT.

...EDNESDAY 24th SEPT.
...AD A GOOD SLEEP. BREAKFAST ON JALAN JAKSA OK. THEN T...
...ANK GOT OUT 500,000 RP! A HALF MILLIONAIRE. WADS OF
...NE STUFF. THEN TO McDONALDS AT DEPT. STORE. SHAKE. DOUGH
...HAT 15,000. GOOD HANDICRAFTS SECTION. JOE PROBLEMS
...AIN WITH AMEX. WENT OFF IN TAXI TO GET MONEY.
...GOT BUS TO OLD BATAVIA. (LOST AFANGS IN DEPT. STORE.)
...ENT TO WAYANG MUSEUM IN OLD DUTCH HOUSE.
...E HOUSE MORE INTERESTING THAN EXHIBITS.
...HEN OVER TO EX-CITY HALL. FEW MAPS AND FURNITU...

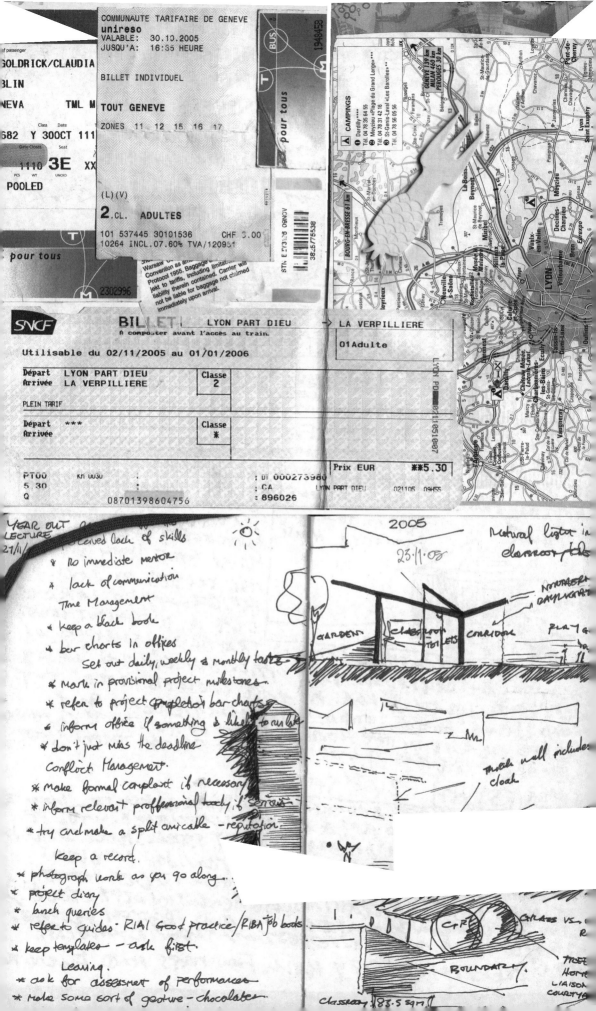

COMMUNAUTE TARIFAIRE DE GENEVE
unireso
VALABLE: 30.10.2005
JUSQU'A: 16:35 HEURE

BILLET INDIVIDUEL

TOUT GENEVE

ZONES 11 12 15 16 17

2.CL. ADULTES

101 537445 30101536   CHF 3.00
10264 INCL.07.60% TVA/120951

GOLDRICK/CLAUDIA
BLIN
NEVA   TML M
682 Y 300CT 111
1110 3E XX
POOLED

Warsaw Convention as amended by the Hague
Protocol 1955. Baggage liability limited unless a higher value is
ject to tariffs, including limitations therein
liability therein contained. Carrier will
not be liable for baggage not claimed
immediately upon arrival.

SNCF   BILLET   LYON PART DIEU → LA VERPILLIERE
A composter avant l'accès au train.

01Adulte

Utilisable du 02/11/2005 au 01/01/2006

| Départ | LYON PART DIEU | Classe |
| Arrivée | LA VERPILLIERE | 2 |

PLEIN TARIF

| Départ | *** | Classe |
| Arrivée | | * |

Prix EUR **5.30

PT00   KM 0030
5 30   : DI 000273980
Q   : CA   LYON PART DIEU   021105 09H55
        08701398604756   : 896026

---

received lack of skills

* no immediate mentor
* lack of communication
Time Management
* keep a black book
* bar charts in offices
    Set out daily, weekly & monthly tasks
* Mark in provisional project milestones.
* refer to project completion bar charts
* inform office if something is likely to run late
* don't just miss the deadline
Conflict Management.
* make formal complaint if necessary
* inform relevant professional body if serious
* try and make a split amicable - reputation.
    keep a record.
* photograph work as you go along
* project diary
* bunch queries
* refer to guides- RIAI Good practice/RIBA job books
* keep templates - ask first.
    Leaving.
* ask for assessment of performance
* make some sort of gesture - chocolates.

2005
23.11.05

Natural light in classrooms

NORTHERN DAYLIGHT
GARDEN CLASSROOM CORRIDOR PLAYG
TOILETS

Finish wall include cloak

CtR
GLASS VS.

BOUNDARY

TREE HOME LIAISON COURTYARD

Classroom 83.5 sqm

Amsterdam 1999.

Beurs - HP Berlage.   Amsterdam
Schroeder House - Rietveld   Utrecht
Kiefhoek Estate and Church - JJP Oud
Rotterdam
Kunsthal - Rotterdam - 1987/92 Koolhaas
Wozoco's Apartment for Elderly People MVRDV
Amsterdam 94/97
Villa VPRO Hilversum 1993/97   MVRDV
Double House Utrecht 95/97 MVRDV
Educatorium Utrecht 93/97 Koolhaas
Minnaert Building Utrecht - 94/98 Neutelings
                                              Riedijk
Maastricht · Academy for Health + Architecture
Wiel Arets · 89/93
20 Apartments for the Elderly · Maastricht ·92/94 _Wiel
Apartment Tower KNSM Islands 90/96 Wiel Arets
Claus en Kaan

Van Nelle Factory Rotterdam · Brinkman Van de
                                                      Shaw

Senor Magugalli   Cornel
                                      Rome
Liverani Molteni - 23.2.05
Liverani-Pironi Architecture Foundation
London.
2 Renzo Market
Scorgno - Pavilion 1999-2003
House 1 2004
① Clear connection to the site
② Scale ⟶ (Architecture)
③ Forms + Shapes simple - simplicity - Rules
④ Conception + Abstraction
     Abstract Model or Archetype
Economy - not to waste space
                    Like money
Relationship between fields + markets.

Always excellent   lots of
                                      ideas
Empire process — obvious

✱ Rationalise ⟶ Corbusier collaborators ℞
- Reduce ⟶ Jacobsen.
Shores/Vegghani

8

The impact of photography on building design
ROS KAVANAGH

Architecture and photography.

In 1851, the French Commission des Monuments Historiques realised the importance of a newly developed technology, photography, and commissioned several photographers to document the monument stock across the country. They hoped to speed up the work already in hand, leapfrogging the teams of surveyors laden down with levels, rulers and drawing boards. The intention was to produce accurate representations of all the national monuments in a timescale never before achieved. It has been suggested that, much more than any measured drawing, the photographs portrayed the monuments in a subjective manner. The photographs ranged from romantic views taken during dramatic sunsets, to bleached out shadowless forms captured in the noonday sun. The hundreds of images created in the Mission Héliographique's short life had become records of the photographers' intentions, not an objective catalogue as the Commission had hoped.

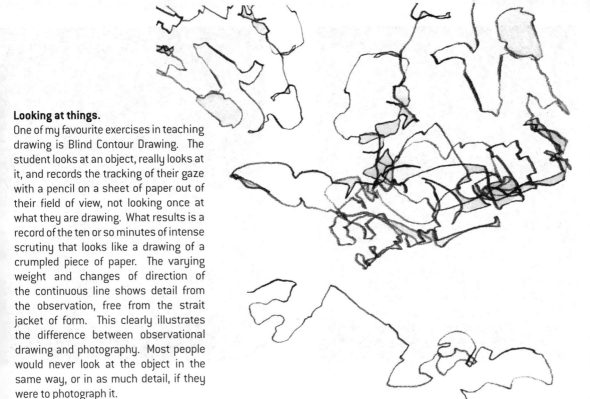

Looking at things.

One of my favourite exercises in teaching drawing is Blind Contour Drawing. The student looks at an object, really looks at it, and records the tracking of their gaze with a pencil on a sheet of paper out of their field of view, not looking once at what they are drawing. What results is a record of the ten or so minutes of intense scrutiny that looks like a drawing of a crumpled piece of paper. The varying weight and changes of direction of the continuous line shows detail from the observation, free from the strait jacket of form. This clearly illustrates the difference between observational drawing and photography. Most people would never look at the object in the same way, or in as much detail, if they were to photograph it.

Blow – up.

A photograph is of course capable of showing very high levels of detail, limited only by the capture method and the form of presentation. The advertising industry has given photographers new technologies where it has become very easy (if expensive!) to produce detailed images several meters across. Looking at an image in a gallery, say by Andreas Gursky, the sheer level of detail gives you a giddy exhilaration. Most photographic images have been projected by a lens onto a flat plane, film or digital sensor, fixing the relative positions of the viewer and subject in perpetuity with the image. It's sometimes frustrating when trying to look at a subject in a photographic image that you, the viewer, are continuously stuck in a position which has been pre-determined.

Different ways of looking.

A very precise spatial relationship between the observer and the observed is contained in any photograph. This way of imaging, being akin to our natural visual perception, has had pre – eminence since the renaissance in Western Europe. The origins of this mortal's perspective (as opposed to an all seeing god's eye view for example) may owe more to optical technology than we think. The Venetians being expert in glass production, had ample opportunity to develop and use concave mirrors which could be used as an aid for painting. Any challenge to this orthodoxy still has the power to shock. Picasso's "Les Demoiselles d'Avignon" taken purely as an exercise in representation, steps neatly outside the narrow corridor linking one eye to a subject. Photography and film have also managed to play with these rules in small but successful ways.

Superimpose the stereo images above on each other by crossing your eyes!

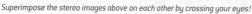

The design process.

Drawing occupies an unassailable position as being the prime activity employed by an architect to express and document every step of the design process. Photography, however can be extremely useful as part of any analysis in this. Examples include; site analysis, context surveys etc. It has been used as a way to inform concept generation, composition and material usage by many architects. Enric Miralles cut elements from photos to accentuate the remainder, with the white negative presence of what was removed still exerting a more malleable influence, open to modification. I remember an AA book from the 80s ("Temple Island" by Michael Webb 1987) where all the shadows in one photograph were cut out... making white shadows, this inversion being useful in looking at the context in a more open fashion. The sheer accident of taking a photograph provides information to pore over later at the drawing board, while more recently, easier to use computer programs provide ample opportunity to cannabalise images for design or presentation. This use of 2d images mapped on to a virtual 3d form relies very much on the seductiveness of the image, an addition to its implied verite.

Thoughts on a page.

Drawing can be a mainly personal exercise, those scribbles mean more to their creator than anyone else, but a photographic image is instantly communicable and interpretable, being a vehicle for the ideas it represents, contains or implies. The camera can be successfully used as a sketching tool, creating compositions, colour ratios and accidental load-stones of concept. Most of all, it is a great tool for capturing and expressing emotion, something easily forgotten or suppressed at a project's detailed design stage.

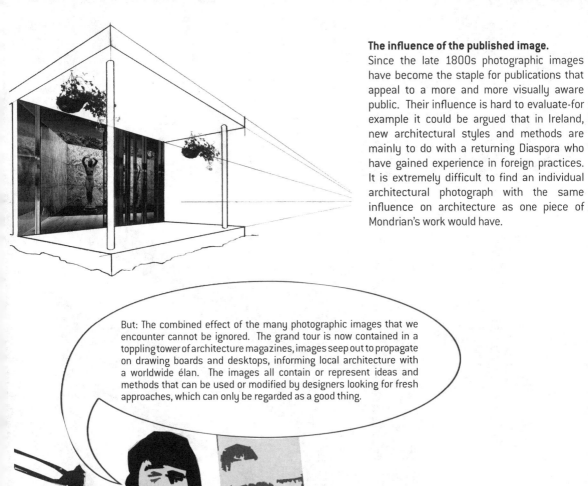

The influence of the published image.
Since the late 1800s photographic images have become the staple for publications that appeal to a more and more visually aware public. Their influence is hard to evaluate-for example it could be argued that in Ireland, new architectural styles and methods are mainly to do with a returning Diaspora who have gained experience in foreign practices. It is extremely difficult to find an individual architectural photograph with the same influence on architecture as one piece of Mondrian's work would have.

But: The combined effect of the many photographic images that we encounter cannot be ignored. The grand tour is now contained in a toppling tower of architecture magazines, images seep out to propagate on drawing boards and desktops, informing local architecture with a worldwide élan. The images all contain or represent ideas and methods that can be used or modified by designers looking for fresh approaches, which can only be regarded as a good thing.

Bleaching.
One possible indication of photography having a direct impact on architecture would be the cumulative effects that many cycles of building and photographing buildings have produced over the last century. When a room is photographed, the junk is taken away, the pictures are straightened, and the photographer tries to give an idea of the geometry of the room. This is most easily achieved by simplifying the scene so that the space can be easily read in one image. The photographer is certainly most complicit, but who is to say that, in emulating previous examples of work seen through photographs, that the architect does not simplify or rationalize a new design to achieve this perfection a little more easily? This effect could be termed "bleaching" as it represents the washing away of detail and complication, leaving only the strong geometric elements courting themselves over acres of flat white surfaces.

Make believe worlds.
Coming out of the cinema after having seen the new Harry Potter film, to the main outdoor plaza in a new shopping centre, I was struck by the similarity of the two experiences. You are immersed in an environment where there is a tremendous amount of effort expended to make you feel celebrated, entertained and cosseted. This was perhaps accentuated by all of the Christmas lights spread over the trees and facades. But with gushing fountains and a tv screen with synched sound playing to the shoppers, it seemed as if our built environment was taking its cue from our virtual experience. This has already accustomed us to the new, softening its impact as it eventually appears in the flesh.

Ros Kavanagh began practice in 1997 as an architectural photographer. He also works collaboratively with artists and curators, theatre and dance performers, designers and directors, documenting exhibitions, installations and stage performances.

Gedenkenskirche
Berlin.

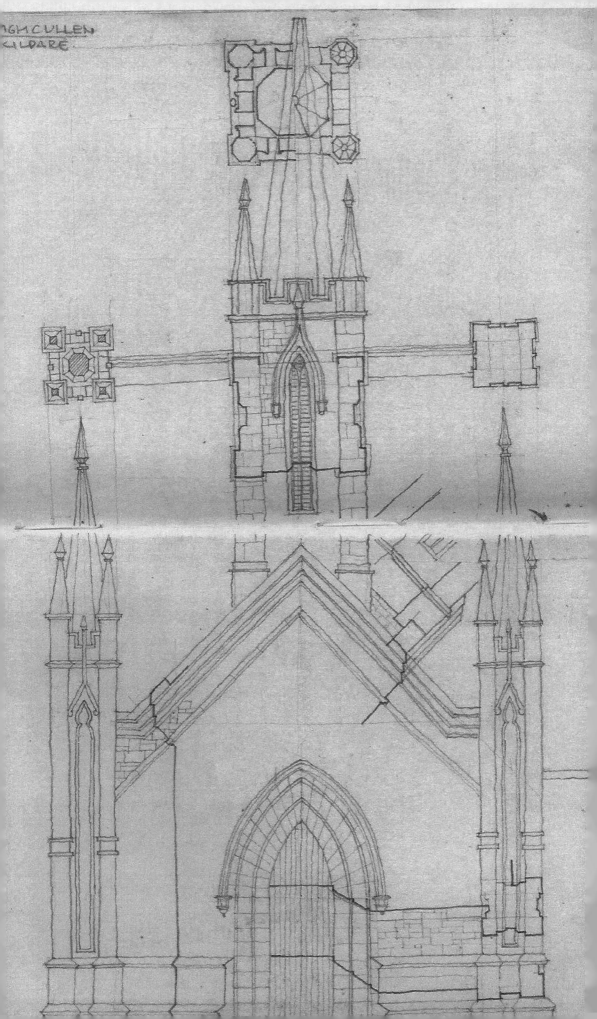

GHCULLEN
KILDARE.

TALLAGHT

ARCH

CORBEL

KEVIN'S
NDALOUGH

ARCH

CORBEL

ST MARY'S
CHAPEL OF EASE
BLACK CHURCH)

PAZZI CHAPEL
TUESDAY PM
2·4·91

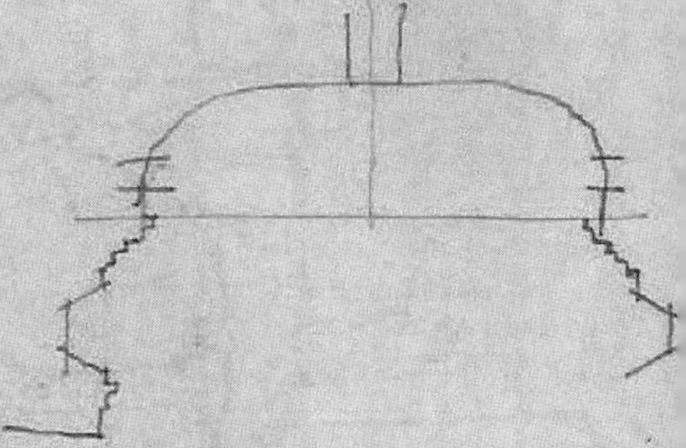

• stained glass
  behind altar
  roundel + rectang
• white stucco wall
• grey stone pilaste
  mouldings, coffe
  aedicules.

• roundels - glazed
  blue terracco &
  white statues;
  grey surrounds;

• blue frieze (hair
  blue inner don
  • lancet fram
    as S. Spirito

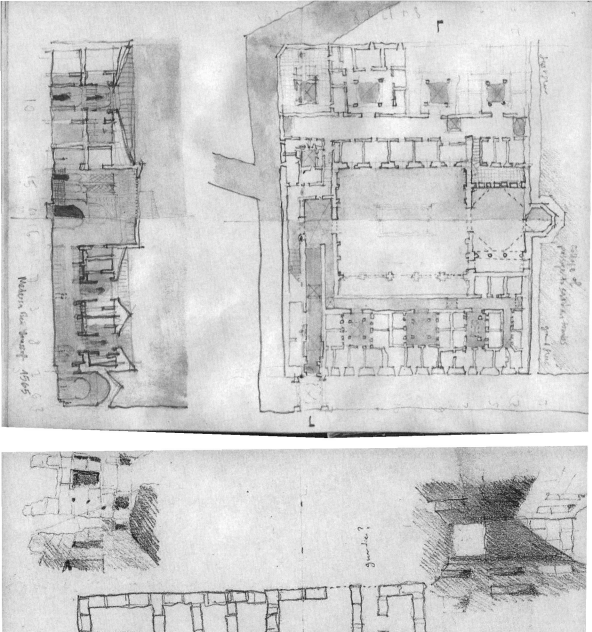

Modern Har Janszk 1565

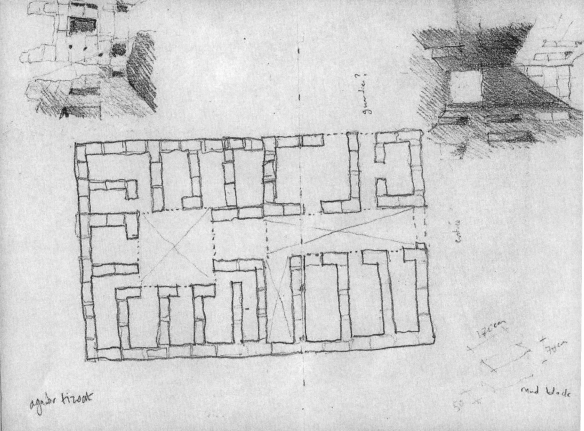

agadir tizzat

garden?

centre

170cm

70cm

50

Mud Wade

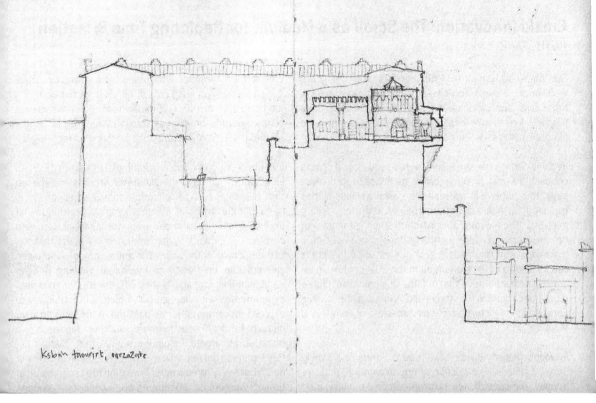

Ksbah taourirt, oarzazate

agadir construit 1026 ~~(fortes arabesque?)~~
  disused 1950 after gradual decline
  people now keep wheat/sorghum in older
  houses (many have built new houses)

- deposit basins loaned a mug of grain for every bag taken out
- guardian lived over entrance
- each village had a room and a key - each door had
  a wooden lock

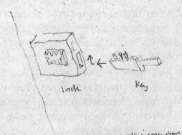

locks   key

guardian's room above

prison   storage unit   deposit basins   porch

grand agadir à amezri → fonctionne toujours
agadir à   tizgé à dans une grotte

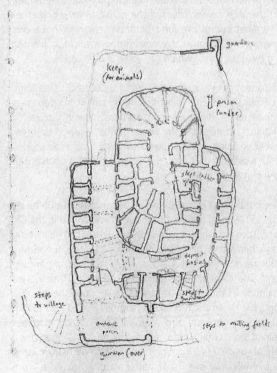

keep
(for animals)

guardian

prison
(under)

steps (taller)

deposit
basins

steps to
guardian

steps
to village

entrance
porch

guardian (over)

steps to milling fields

Emaki innovation: The Scroll as a Medium for Depicting Time & Motion
RUTH STARR

The physical format in which artists and designers work often informs, inhibits or facilitates their design. Notebooks, sketchbooks, indeed canvases have obvious physical limits, whereas the scroll, in theory, can be almost limitless - at least along one axis.

In considering the possibilities released to designers choosing to work in scroll format as opposed to book or page, this paper will address the narrative possibilities exploited by Asian artists in their visual story telling pursuits. These methods reached their pinnacle of development in 12th century Japan but declined thereafter, yet the ancient techniques used in scrolls can be said to have re-emerged in the 20th century in an entirely new medium – that of film. This point is explored by the Japanese art historian Tsuji Nobuo in his essay, *Early Medieval Picture Scrolls as Ancestors of Anime[i] and Manga[ii]*:

In Japan the scroll was held in both hands and slowly unrolled (exposing a section of approximately 50 cm at a time). The pace of viewing and therefore the unfolding of narrative time was entirely in the viewers control. The section rolled in by the right hand becomes the hidden past while the section unfurled by the left hand holds the unseen future. The image before the viewer, expressing imaginary time, intersects with the passage of real time in the physical handling of the scroll. However whether the illustrations are long or short, they all have one element in common: a leftward momentum established by the direction in which the scroll is unrolled.[iii]

Japanese artists were particularly successful at realising the possibilities of hand scrolls or emaki for depicting moments of deep emotion and fast flowing dramatic action.[iv] In addition, the *emaki* format allowed painters great flexibility and the freedom to spin out their stories with a graphic ingenuity not equalled until the advent of the motion picture.

The hand scroll was in common use throughout China by the 1st century and was introduced into Japan in the 6th or 7th century along with Buddhism. *Emaki* can be literally translated as 'rolled object with pictures,' containing illustrations that tell a story, often with accompanying text. The format, considered one of the high points of painting in the native Japanese style, flourished during both the Heian and Kamakura periods (794AD – 1333AD). The *emaki* consists of numerous pieces of silk or paper joined horizontally and rolled around a cylinder. They are around 20 to 50 cm high and can be up to 20m long, with individual sheets of paper varying in width from one scroll to another and joined by a narrow overlap. The papers were usually made either from the bark of a mulberry tree or thin rice paper from the Wickstroemia canescens. The number of scrolls making up an *emaki* set may vary from one or two to as many as forty eight.

It is interesting to note how Tsuji relates that in 1999 an exhibition in Chiba City Museum of Art, Japan explored the coincidences of pictorial conventions of early hand scrolls and the cinematographic techniques of *anime*. A leading Japanese animator Takahata Isao, who curated the exhibition, demonstrated his belief that the contemporary enthusiasm for anime among Japanese viewers can be traced to modes of viewing images established as far back as the 12th century, 'when artists experimented with sophisticated pictorial techniques to express movement and the passage of time in narrative picture scrolls.'[v] Furthermore, another Japanese art historian Minamoto Toyomune argues that 'historically the Japanese did not appear to perceive space in terms of depth but interpreted it more in relation to a progression of time.'[vi] Western commentators often describe Japanese paintings as flat, lacking in three dimensional depth, but this is to ignore the fact that artists intentionally strove to eliminate depth.

It is worth considering that until modern times Japanese paintings were executed by applying silk and water soluble colours with animal hair brushes to paper or silk. These materials greatly influenced the results and there was no way to correct or repaint an unsatisfactory area. Unlike pencil on paper, or oil on canvas, a line or colour on paper or silk could not be changed, and consequently artists had to plan the entire painting before they could start, rather than allow the design to evolve as they went along. Once a single stroke of the brush was made, every other brushstroke had to be balanced with it until the painting was finished. This inability to correct made painting more difficult yet also had advantages, since great skill with the brush was required knowing that a single weak or irrelevant stroke could ruin a painting. [vii] As a result, Japanese paintings tend to be fresh and lively, often with a feeling of spontaneity, a characteristic present in hand scrolls.

The Miraculous Tales Of Mount Shigi
A good example of ink drawings where the narrative is depicted in a continuous compositional technique in which scenes flow from one to the other is *The Miraculous Tales of Mount Shigi (Shigisan engi emaki)*. It does not depend on its text to convey the narrative, but rather deploys images to capture and refocus the

viewer's attention. The scrolls are classic early examples of a religious *emaki* illustrating an *enji* or the founding of a temple. They depict miracles associated with the Priest Myúren, the founder of the temple. The three scrolls together include four text sections, but rather than relying on words the illustrations are quite self explanatory once the basic outlines of the story are known. The illustrations are drawn in grey ink under a light colour wash enabling the ink outlines to show through the wash. The energy and vivacity of the human figures is achieved through this emphasis on the ink line.

Movement

The opening scene of the first scroll is commonly known as *The Flying Granary Story*. Through the power of his faith, Myúren was able to send the granary flying through the air on top of his begging bowl. *Fig 1* shows a humorous depiction of a startled group watching the rice granary starting to shake as the golden alms bowl flies out from within. What seem like almost ethereal lines have been drawn to suggest the bowl is moving through the air, whilst most of the granary is out of the picture frame suggesting it is hovering at a great height. The squire on horseback and the local peasants are shown in comic bewilderment as they chase after the bowl. Everything revealed as this scroll unrolls — people, warehouse, water, - is imbued with a strong sense of movement rendered with restless strokes of the brush and with very thin, pale colouring. This is another facet of the Japanese native style, 'one which stressed dynamic action and a rustic boisterous mood.' [viii]

Multiple Exposure

An interesting technique used in the third scroll of *The Miraculous Tales of Mount Shigi* might be thought a precursor to the technique known in photography today as 'multiple exposure.' It shows the journey of Myúren's sister, a Buddhist nun, in search of her long lost brother which eventually takes her to the Great Buddha Hall of the Todaiji in Nara. Here the nun spends the night praying in front of the statue of the Great Buddha. While the background of the Great Buddha hall remains stationary, we see the nun at various stages of the night - kneeling in prayer, sleeping, and then setting off in the morning. As the reader unfolds this scroll, the miniscule nun is found moving forward through a misty landscape. Finally the viewer is confronted suddenly by the image — 'similar to a cinematic pan shot — of a sacred mountain surrounded by wondrous swirls of colourful cloud.' [ix]

The Tale Of Genji

The oldest, and widely considered the most splendid, of *emaki* extant from the Heian times are *The Tale of Genji*

scrolls. The novel was written in the 12th century AD and has been called the first great novel in world history. It describes the life and loves of an one-time prince, know from his family name, 'the shining Genji.' There may originally have been as many as twenty of these scrolls but only four have survived, probably painted sometime around the mid twelfth century. Despite lacking the horizontal flow of movement developed in subsequent *emaki* (the Genji Scrolls consist of separate scenes with sections of text interspersed among them), these scrolls have considerable artistic impact.

Colour

The most important of these impacts is perhaps the lavish use of thick colours, carefully selected to enhance the mood of each scene. Mineral pigments such as bright red, green and blue were used alongside gold and silver for a lavish effect, and the costumes and furnishings were decorated with delicate patterns. Production of the paintings was probably a group project – 'a manufactured painting,' with a supervising artist drawing outlines in Indian ink and his assistants painting in the colours. This technique was used with great success in the Heian and Kamakura periods for illustrating romantic tales.

Internal Axonometrics

A distinctive technical convention familiar to modern architects is used in the Genji scrolls: the removal of roofs from buildings to provide axonometric views into their interiors from above. Another convention is the drawing of faces with stylized 'straight lines for eyes and hooks for noses.' The most important theme within *The Tale of Genji* – the concept of *mono no aware*, best translated as 'the pathos of things' or 'the moving quality of experience' – is not an easy idea to convey visually. The artists who planned the compositions used pictorial conventions, possibly invented by them, that were particularly effective in illustrating moments of high emotional intensity. The cutaway axonometric view was used not just to depict an indoor activity in an outdoor setting, but the odd angles created by the walls, sliding doors and folding screens when seen from above were visual metaphors for the emotions felt by the characters in the illustrations. The absence or presence of a space in which the figures could move also contributes insight into their feelings. Colour and pattern heighten the mood of the scene. All these elements taken together create for the viewer a strong impression of *mono no aware* – 'whether it be the pleasure one experiences looking at a garden bathed in moonlight and hearing the sound of someone playing the flute, or the pain one feels at the thought of losing a loved one.' [x]

Space and Emotion

An example of this type of composition is the first illustration for the chapter *Kashiwagi*, in which the retired emperor visits his daughter who, having betrayed her husband Genji, has decided to become a nun. *(Fig two)* In this treatment, the roofs of buildings are omitted to produce clear overhead views of the inhabitants. The steep diagonal lines of the architecture, crossed at many different angles by the screens set up around the lady, emphasise the conflicting emotions of the characters.

In addition, the Genji scroll illustrates how flexible the scroll format can be in conveying emotional discomfort through compositional devices. In the scene where Genji is aware that his wife's attendants know that he is not the child's father, his emotional disquiet is suggested by physical awkwardness of his placement at the top of the very sharply slanting floor. Furthermore, the space he occupies is so constricted that even if he wished to raise his head from the baby in his arms, he could not do so. In this scene the architecture plays a key role, at first interrupting the leftward momentum of the illustration and at the same time shielding the figures from view. 'It suggests guilty knowledge that reverberates throughout the room during the ceremony, not only of the wife's adultery but also of Genji's cuckolding of his father many years before. [...] it forces Genji into a cramped position, [...suggesting] the pressure of society coercing him to put a good face on a bad situation.' [xi]

The Tale Of The Major Counsellor Ban

A scroll with perhaps a higher degree of realism than either Shigisan or Genji, and with a deeper understanding of psychological interaction between figures is The Tale of the Major Counsellor Ban *(Ban Dainagon ekotoba)*. It is dated to the second half of the 12th century AD. In three scrolls, the work presents a continuous pictorial narrative of over 6 metres in length and is considered to be one of the finest surviving examples of narrative depiction in this medium. The story is based on an event in the year 866AD when the Ótemmon, the gate inside the imperial compound in Kyúto, burned mysteriously. Ban Dainagon, Major-Counsellor accused his political rival Minamoto no Makoto of arson. Eventually when it is revealed that it was Ban and his son who set the fire, they and other members of their family are exiled.[xii]

As Tsuji points out, in the second scroll, there is an interesting use of a technique 'similar to flashback used in film.'[xiii] A member of Makoto's household runs in panic through the gate, then attendants come into view to announce the news of a pardon for the maligned minister. Inside the gate we see Makoto in the garden protesting his innocence to the gods, followed by a scene of ladies of the household crying. *(Fig 4)* Some women appear to be relieved, implying they already know of the pardon. Thus in one single scene the viewer sees the many changing emotions of the women ranging from despair to hope over a short period of time.

The Book

Emaki produced after the 12th century drew on the successes of the above and other scrolls, using similar pictorial conventions suggesting motion, and developing them further. But treatments of time were not developed. Eventually 'simultaneous depiction technique' seems to have been abandoned altogether, maybe it was considered ineffectual. Individual scenes were separated by passages of texts. Time sequences in *emaki* were depicted more literally after the 12th century resulting in a loss of narrative flow, which might be said to limit the viewer's imagination.

From this time onwards the advantage of the scroll over book format became less obvious to Eastern artists. With the introduction of new technologies in woodblock printing, printed books began to replace hand scrolls. By the seventeenth century woodblock printed books were mass produced and catered for popular tastes and trends rather than the just religious, romantic or historical themes of hand scrolls, which previously were only enjoyed by a limited audience. The scroll had become overlooked. It was not until the 20th century that the scroll's narrative possibilities of unfurling simultaneous depictions of time were rediscovered, this time in the medium of film.

Ruth Starr lectures in the History of Japanese Art, Trinity College Dublin,. She has a Masters degree in the History of Japanese Art from School of Oriental and African Studies (SOAS) at the University of London. She has worked as Cultural Officer with the Embassy of Japan in London.

i Anime is the Japanese abbreviation of the word for animation used to describe popular animated films
iiManga is the Japanese term for 'random sketches' and can also describe comic strip or cartoon.
iii Tsuji, Nobuo. "Early medieval picture scrolls as ancestors of Anime and Manga". Essay in "Births and Rebirths in Japanese Art". Coolidge Rousmaniere, Nicole (ed.). Leiden. Hotei Publishing. 2001. Pg 56
iv Mason, Penelope "History of Japanese art" 2nd edition revised by Dinwiddie, Donald. New Jersey. Pearson Prentice Hall . 2005. Pg 115
v Tsuji.op.cit Pg 53.
vi Ibid. Pg 55
vii Addis, Stephen "How to look at Japanese art". New York. Harry N. Abrams. 1996. Pg. 55
viii Noma, Seiroku "The Arts of Japan, ancient and medieval", Tokyo. Kodansha International. 1996 Pg 151
ix Tsjui. op.cit. Pg 60
x Mason. op.cit Pg 117
xi Ibid. Pg. 118
xii Japan - an illustrated Encyclopaedia. Tokyo. Kodansha 1993 Pg. 97
xiii Ibid Pg 62

NOTES:
A) In this article, Japanese names appear in the traditional style with the family name first and the given name second.
B) For an interactive experience visit "The Illustrated Legends of the Kitano Shrine" (Kitano Tenjin Engi Maki) website hosted by the Metropolitan Museum of Art, New York at http://www.metmuseum.org/explore/kitanomaki/kitano_splash.htm

Fig1. The Flying Granary Story from Shigisan Engi Emaki. The Chōgo Sonshinji.

. The Scene in which Princess Nyosan's father, the real Emperor Suzaku, visits to try to persuade his disconsolate daughter not to withdraw from court life to become a Buddist nun from Genji ᴐogatari Emaki. The Tokogawa Art Museum.

Fig 3. The Opening Scene of the burning of the Ōtenmon Gate from Ban Dainagon Emaki. The Idemitsu Museum of Arts.

11

Sequence
GRIT KOALICK

A single image manifests a particular view of space and time. One can increase its possibilities by placing additional views next to it. A sequence of images allows an understanding to emerge frame by frame.

Similarities between adjacent images contribute towards reading the sequence in four dimensions. Of equal importance though are differences between one image and the next. If one uses the interaction between similarity and difference in a calculated manner, a sequence can become a significant tool for describing the built environment. The use of images and words in parallel allows a message to be communicated precisely.

Text, however, should not be used purely to describe the image. Conversely, images should not serve simply as illustrations to text. In simple sequences the use of text can be limited to indicating abstract ideas, while in more complex ones images need to be connected by passages of text.

This article explores the use of the sequence as a tool capable of describing and/or explaining the built environment of Forst (a small town in East Germany) as the complex result of broad social, economic and political forces acting over time.

Diverse Images
Contemporary Forst could be described by a series of diverse images. In the following selection of images each frame is comparable to a still photograph and illustrates a particular situation at a given point in time. The spatial relationships of these views are left undefined and this makes 'in-between' images impossible to reconstruct.

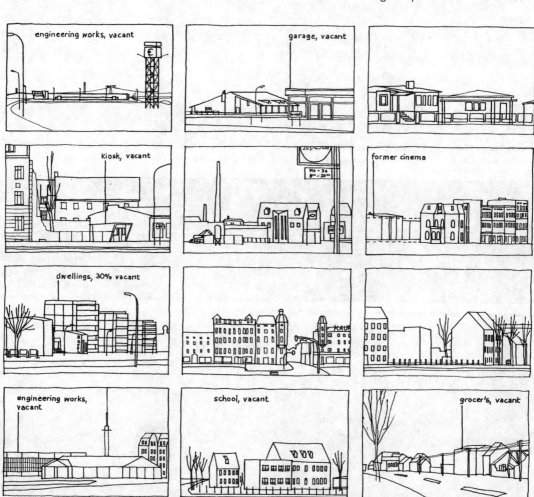

Spatial Sequence

Alternatively, a typical spatial situation within the town centre could be presented using a series of images in which the distance between the viewpoints is diminished. In this case, the constantly changing field of vision strengthens the impression of motion. With the help of still images, the viewer can reconstruct a movement through space and time.

mill C.H.Pürschel

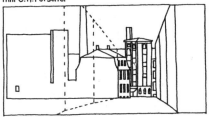   

In describing another location in the town, this more complex arrangement of frames, with more erratic changes in the field of vision, imitates familiar patterns of perception.

marketplace

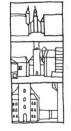 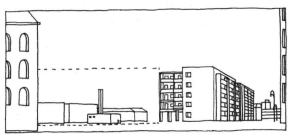 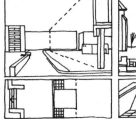 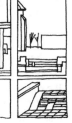

Temporal Sequence

If the field of vision and the framing are fixed a sequence can map the development of a place over time. A few selected images represent aspects of the town at decisive moments in history.

1700

1920

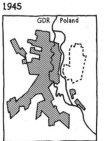
1945 — GDR / Poland

1990 — Germany / Poland

2006 — European Union

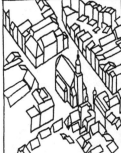
1920

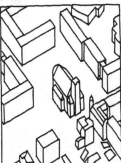
1989

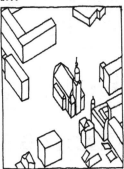
2006

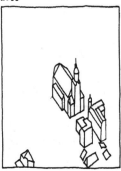
2010

Causal Sequence

The relationship between cause and effect can be described within a unified medium by a combination of diagrams and flat abstract illustrations. Although they don't look like space, charts and maps can contribute to an understanding of space. Their logic, comparability and objectivity help to explain social, economic and political causes, while the use of flat illustrations can portray spatiotemporal effects.

In the 1970s blocks of flats took the place of old buildings in the town centre.

After the wall came down people realized their dreams in the outskirts.

Due to the high rate of unemployment young people in particular leave the town.

1992   16%
2005   27%

In 1991 the average age was 39.2 years; by 2003 it was already 44.

1990   2004

sources: Stadt Forst, www.forst-lausitz.de & www.wikipedia.de

If the current rate of depopulation continues, Forst will be empty in 2065.

Today almost 30 per cent of all dwellings in the town centre are vacant.

While the outskirts grow, the centre disappears.

Space is left for dreams.

Schema

The complex forces that create an urban fabric might be represented with a synthesis of images. This relies on a particular composition to express their interrelations. Text eliminates interpretations and provides instead a more focused idea.

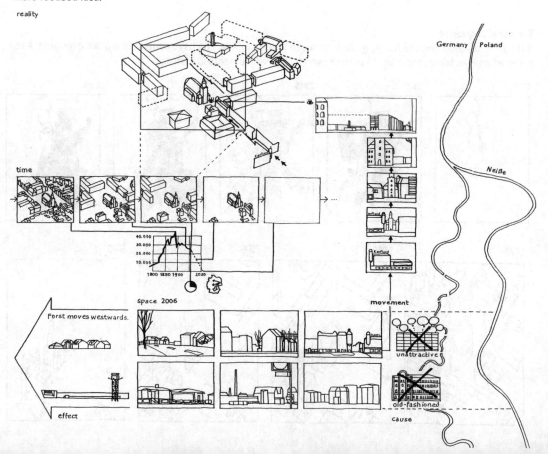

reality

Germany / Poland

time

Neiße

space 2006

movement

Forst moves westwards.

unattractive

old-fashioned

effect

cause

Narration

Alternatively, a narrative could be imposed, allowing a plot to select particular fragments, with the aim of forming a continuous story line of space, time and causality.

Up to the 19th century Forst was a small settlement.

During industrialization the town developed into a German Manchester. The municipal area was enlarged considerably.

Forst was the principal town of the German textile industry.

In World War II 88 per cent of Forst was destroyed.

As a result of the war the town was divided. The German part continued to exist as a wounded town: Even today war damage can be found. The Polish part was completely devastated.

The old buildings that survived World War II were in state of neglect.

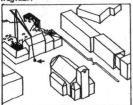

In the 1970s the remaining old buildings in the marketplace were replaced by blocks of flats.

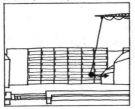
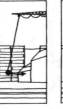

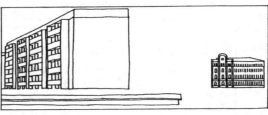

After the wall came down industrial estates were developed in the outskirts of the town.

The textile industry totally collapsed. New firms arose in the early 90s. People hoped.

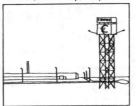

They realized the dream of living in their own homes.

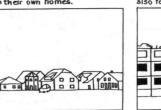

The centre became deserted. The high rate of unemployment also forced people to leave.

2006: Forst is shrinking.

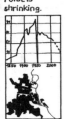

The working-class areas lose one tooth after the other.

The centre consists of unused, undefined space.

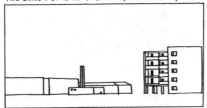

Once valuable old mills were conquered by nature.

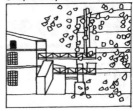

The new generation of buildings will be sold off soon.

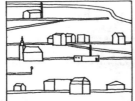

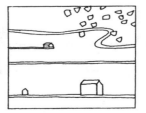

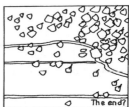

The end?

Grit Koalick is a tutor at TU Dresden, Faculty of Architecture, Chair of Presentation Methods. www.visuranto.de

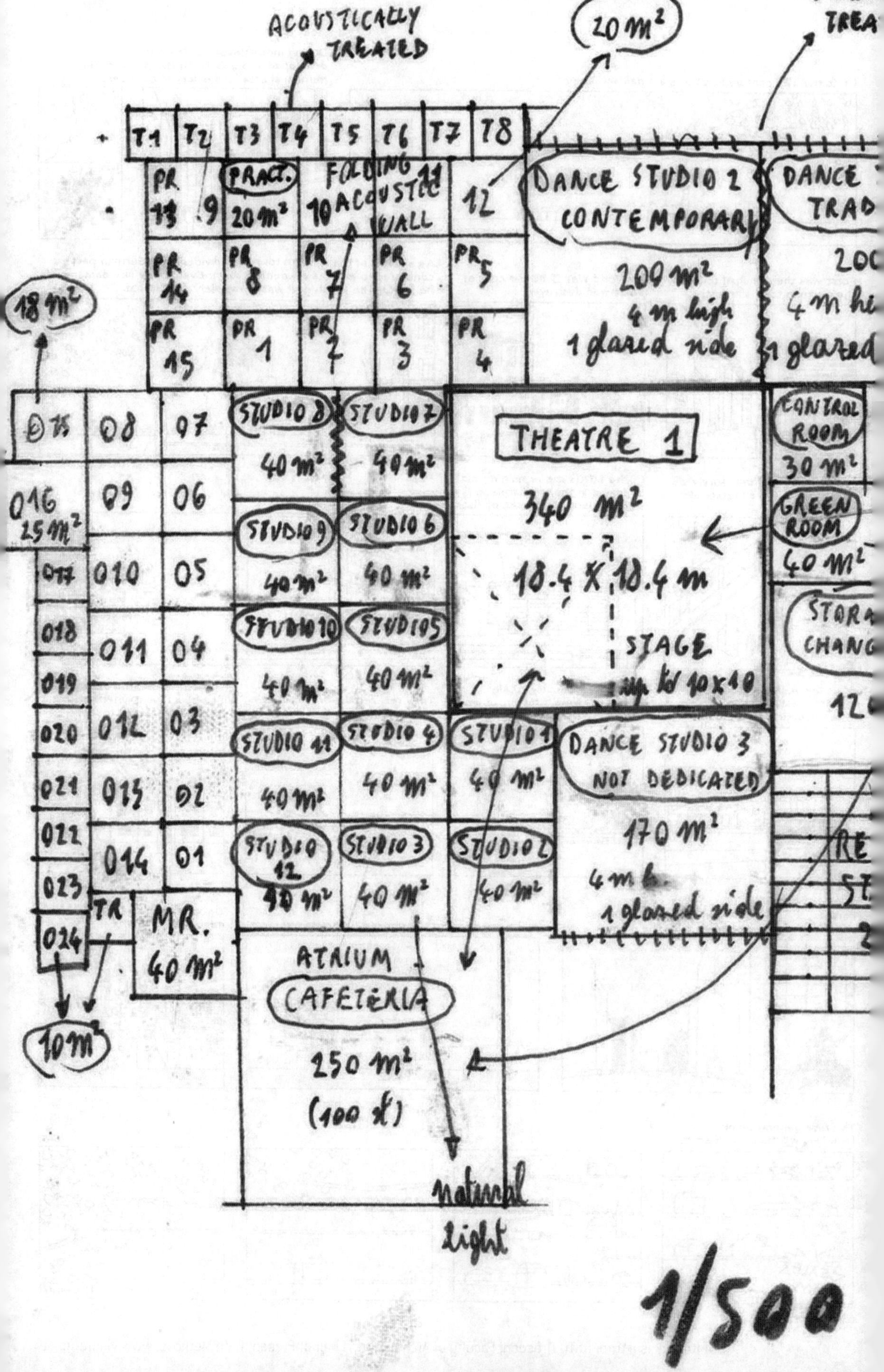

12

ACOUSTICALLY TREATED

20 m²

FOLD TREA

| T.1 | T.2 | T.3 | T.4 | T.5 | T.6 | T.7 | T.8 |

PR 13 — 9 — PRACT. 20 m² — FOLDING 10 ACOUSTIC WALL 11 — 12

DANCE STUDIO 2 CONTEMPORARY
200 m²
4 m high
1 glazed side

DANCE TRAD
200
4 m he
1 glazed

PR 14 — PR 8 — PR 7 — PR 6 — PR 5

PR 15 — PR 1 — PR 2 — PR 3 — PR 4

18 m²

TC — O8 — 97 — STUDIO 8 40 m² — STUDIO 7 40 m²

THEATRE 1
340 m²
18.4 X 18.4 m
STAGE up to 10x10

CONTROL ROOM 30 m²

O16 25 m² — O9 — O6 — STUDIO 9 40 m² — STUDIO 6 40 m²

GREEN ROOM 40 m²

O17 — O10 — O5 — STUDIO 10 40 m² — STUDIO 5 40 m²

STORA CHANG

O18 — O11 — O4 — STUDIO 10 40 m² — STUDIO 5 40 m²

120

O19 — O20 — O12 — O3 — STUDIO 11 40 m² — STUDIO 4 40 m² — STUDIO 1 40 m²

DANCE STUDIO 3 NOT DEDICATED
170 m²
4 m h
1 glazed side

O21 — O13 — O2

O22 — O23 — O14 — O1 — STUDIO 12 40 m² — STUDIO 3 40 m² — STUDIO 2 40 m²

RE ST

O24 — TR — MR. 40 m²

10 m

ATRIUM
CAFETERIA
250 m²
(100 x)

natural light

1/500

COUSTIC

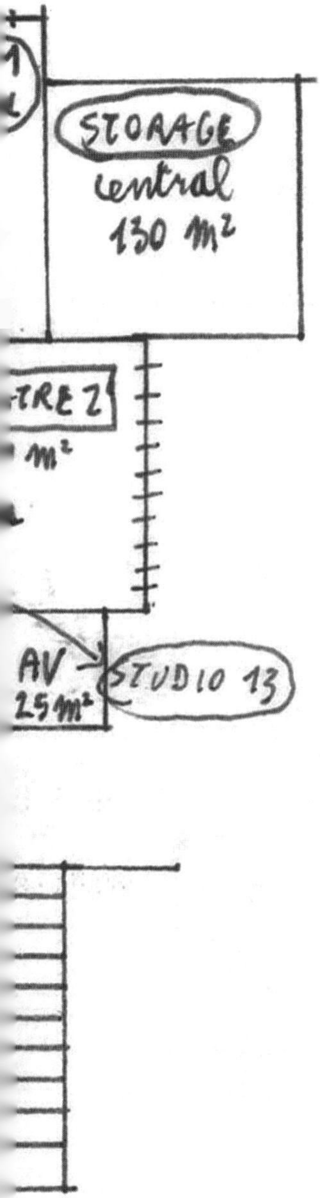

STORAGE
central
130 m²

TRE 2
m²

AV
25 m²   STUDIO 13

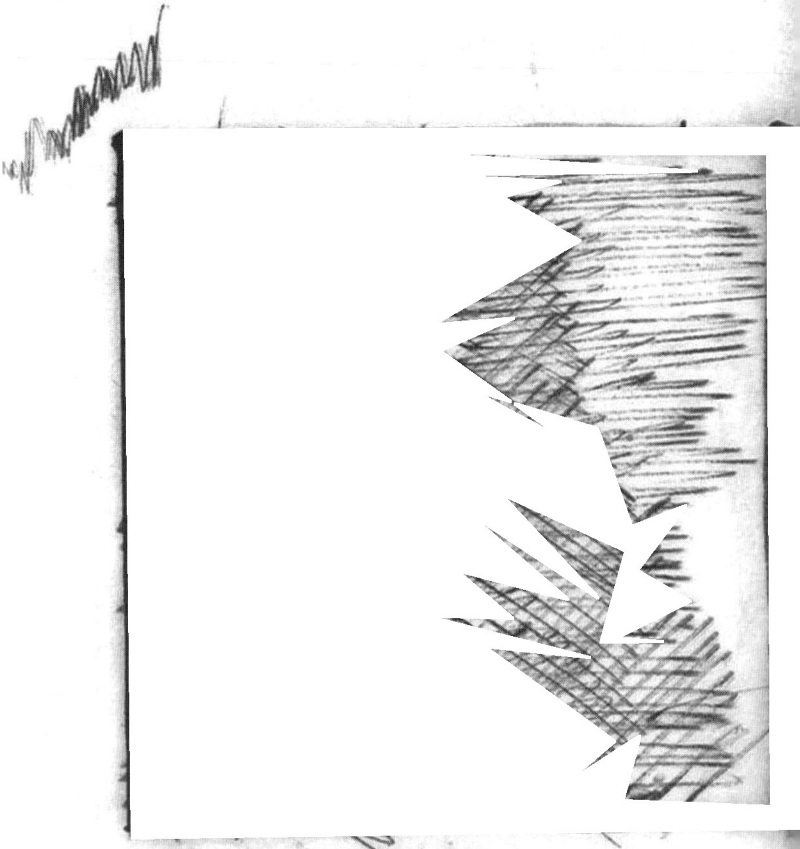

BLACK BOX

BLACK TILES

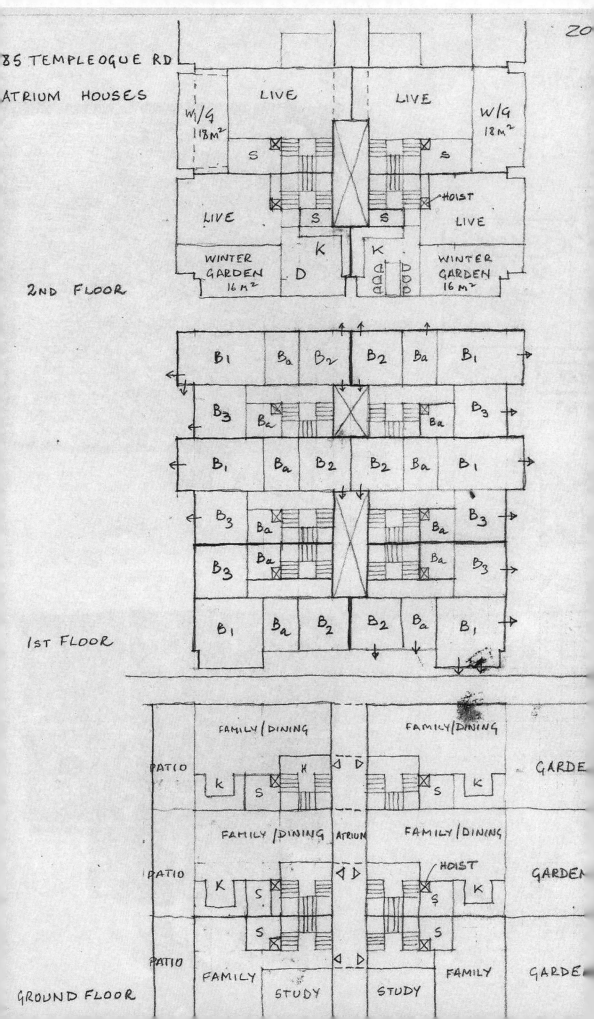

85 TEMPLEOGUE RD

ATRIUM HOUSES

2ND FLOOR

1ST FLOOR

GROUND FLOOR

20

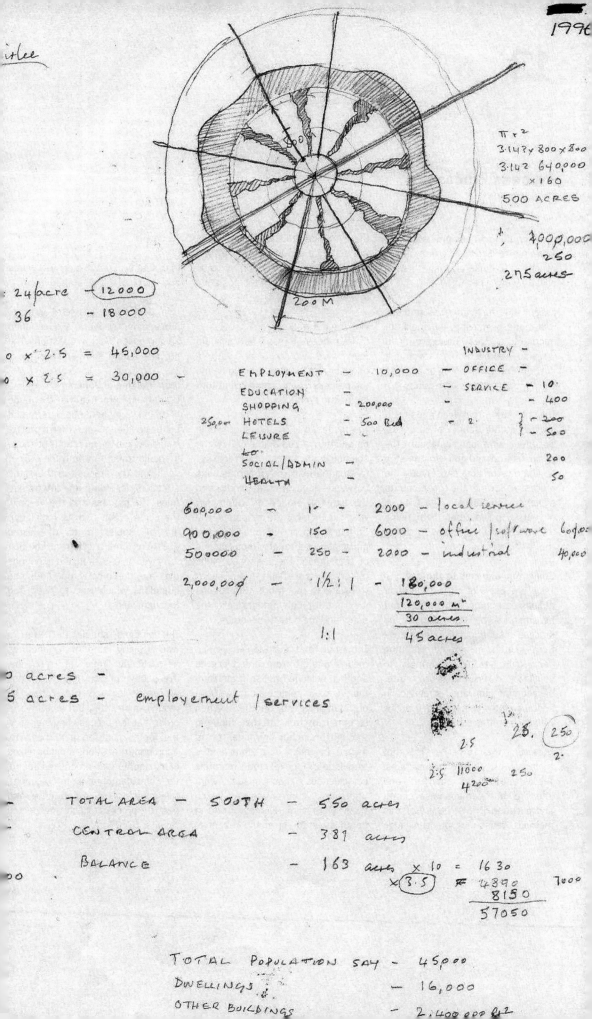

itlee

1996

πr^2
3.143 × 800 × 800
3.142 640,000
× 160
500 ACRES

$\checkmark$ 7,00,000
250
275 acres

: 24/acre — 12000
36 — 18000

0 × 2.5 = 45,000

0 × 2.5 = 30,000 —

INDUSTRY —

EMPLOYMENT	— 10,000	— OFFICE —	
EDUCATION	—	— SERVICE — 10.	
SHOPPING	— 200,000	—	— 400
250,000 HOTELS	— 500 Bed	— 2	} — 200
LEISURE	—		} — 500
SOCIAL/ADMIN	—		200
HEALTH	—		50

600,000	— 1.	— 2000	— local service
900,000	— 150	— 6000	— office / software 60,000
500000	— 250	— 2000	— industrial 40,000
2,000,000	— 1½ : 1	— 180,000	
		120,000 m²	
		30 acres.	
	1 : 1	45 acres	

0 acres —

5 acres — employement / services

2.5   25. 250
2.
2.5 11000 250
4200

TOTAL AREA — 500TH — 550 acres

CENTRAL AREA — 381 acres

BALANCE — 163 acres × 10 = 1630
× 3.5 = 4890   7000
8150
57050

TOTAL POPULATION SAY — 45,000
DWELLINGS — 16,000
OTHER BUILDINGS — 2,400,000 ft²

13

Process Processed
LAURA HARTY

How should I process process?
Adhering to Serra's dictum: 'There is no way to make drawing, there is only drawing', I began.

Essentially the architect's process is a mode of moving, moving from internal to external. There are many ways to approach this movement, but with my questioning of process two opposing stances are taken.

The transition between positions is the quintessence of process, so either you can establish the positions first and go from one step to another, or you can favour the process allowing the positions to somehow punctuate it. The trick is, of course, to keep them both, using the energy of the process to clarify the positions.[i]

Going from one step to another
The process of the architect defines certain positions. These are benchmarks between which the process is set to occur. This process from sketch design to planning permission, tender drawings to construction issues, is a matter of zooming in, and strategically addressing the problems that arrive with each shift in scale.

However, this process is shot through with chance occurrences. These occurrences interject and interfere, but perhaps also clarify and question. The structure of this method is reassuring, one can gauge the distance traveled and predict the distance left to cover. But one must not loose sight of the process in the striving to reach the positions in time.

Walking the walk
If the process is seen as the main focus, we would begin with a question. This question would define the process; the process will in turn define the product.

The response to the question would be an internalized model of how the solution might be realized. Process in this manner explores the connections between your internal world and the external embedded world into which your idea, the response, will fit. It is an act of understanding and participation, through various modes of translation. The response gains materiality and shape through each translation. The more translations it is put through paradoxically the richer and the purer it becomes.

The word for translation in French means a shift from one place to another, while in English translation more usually implies a change from one language to another.[ii] When externalizing an internal thought, through metaphor or model, every aspect partakes in a shift and a translation. Unexpected manifold coincidences thus ensue, work undergoes confrontations, which then favour a more integral and in depth questioning of the response proposed.

In essence, you make up new words and then find out what they mean.

This, I find, is a useful way of proceeding: the work is questioned and proposes it's own questions. The process is then, self-generating.

From Walking to Dancing
Essentially I propose that the mode of processing should be determined by the position taken. When a project is undertaken the questions posed of it should transform both the project itself and the process in the same direction according to determined rules. The process and the graphic, the commission and its realization are all subjected to the same questions until a coherent solution is arrived at. It is, then, the questions that are the modus operandi, the questions which lead to deep and resonant work.

The process should not form a way of doing things that generates a particular type of response, irrespective of the input, if process processes in such a way then the result can be strong but repetitive. In order that the process is generative, the input must be paid heed to. Appropriate questions must be asked of it, appropriate processes found, the coincidental taken into account, these factors must influence and push the process to yield unexpected results.

In the work of Sophie Calle this juxtaposition between position, process and processed is addressed. Her position is to pose a challenge, and as she proceeds with the challenge, documenting her process, the challenge itself becomes processed, questioned and translated.

Shortly after agreeing to write on process I went to see *Forced Entertainment's* version of Sophie Calle's text *Exquisite Pain* in the Project.[iii] Knowing nothing other than the slightly unsettling title and the beguiling red telephone on the poster, I persuaded a girl in red tights to join me at the performance.

The room was dark, the bleachers clattering. For over two hours without an interval, a man and a woman sat side by side at small tables, screens illuminating alternately over each of their heads as they recounted their tale.

The woman began. The screen above showing a picture of the red phone, on a floral bedspread, in an anonymous room, she told a story of her stay in a hotel room in New Dehli, waiting on a lover that was never to arrive. When she finished the man began to speak, outlining the time when he had suffered most. Then she began again telling her story afresh, until when finished, a new voice registered from the man's side documenting another story, from another world.

Exquisite Pain continues in this fashion, the same story is told repeatedly, morphing slightly each time, interspersed with other people's similarly themed stories. Through the consistent re-telling of the story, this constant play between constants and variables Calle reaches resolution. By going through the same repeated actions and recording each in turn, she performs an act of absolution, of moving on. She moves ahead by constantly revisiting the situation. The various tellings of her tale send her by turns, reeling, raving, weeping, joking. In some tellings she omits details, in others, new ones come to the front. We see that in every story there are facets suitable to reveal to some, and more to others. Perhaps on some reelings we disclose facets from ourselves. It is only through the repeated actions of telling the story that the breadth and weight of the experience is instilled in us, interspersed and interwoven with tales of others' suffering, shunting our view, realigning our understanding for the inevitable retelling of the first.

The logic appears truly modern, the monotony and the repetition leading to a new solution, a way forward. Being at once, current, new and transient,[iv] this manner of processing her experience, through reliving the deep dredge memory and the memories of the previous re-tellings, is both process and product.

Process here is a way of following an idea, documenting its progress, stopping when it stops, letting it disappear in order to find it again. Inevitably the idea will, if it has a strong enough identity, be recognized amidst the crowds.

I think the work of Calle is of special significance in addressing the question of process with an architect's hat on. Our work is far from immediate, we are constantly embroiled in acts of telling and re-telling, of translating and testing. The incidents that intersperse the work also impact the work and are as much part of its fabric as the materials that make it up and the coincidences which tie it together.

It is in the translation of her internal model that the external model is arrived at. This translation is what fixes it to a time, a place.

Laura Harty has studied in UCD and KTH, Stockholm. She works with Lotus Architects.

i Merce Cunningham in conversation with Jacqueline Lesschave-paraphrased.

ii M/M (Paris) *Translation* exhibition, Palais de Tokyo, June 23-September 18, 2005.

iii *Forced Entertainment*, Director: Tim Etchells, *Project Arts Centre*, 20-21 January 2006.

iv Hide Heynen, *Architecture and Modernity*

14

Eucalyptus (latinised from Gr. *eu*, well, *kalypotos*, covered)
LINDSAY JOHNSTON

Plato, following from Socrates, initiated the great Graeco-Roman tradition of *either/or* which has dominated western civilisation since. In *Republic*, Book VI, Plato draws a 'divided line' which sections off the correct vision of knowledge *(episteme)* from the false vision of mere opinion *(doxa)*. He places reason in the highest section of the 'divided line' and imagination in the lowest. Whereas reason *(nous)* is accredited with the capacity to contemplate truth, imagination is relegated to the most inferior form of human opinion - what Plato calls *eikasia* or illusion. Only reason can access the transcendental Ideas. Imagination reflects only the things of our sensory world and is denounced by Plato as an agency of falsehood.[i]

The Greater Blue Mountains region, west of Sydney, Australia, has been designated a World Heritage Area because of its diverse communities of eucalypt forests. It is also famous for its dramatic scenery and is one of the primary tourist destinations in New South Wales. The NSW National Parks and Wildlife Service plans to build a 'Greater Blue Mountains World Heritage Area Visitor Centre' on a site at Bilpin on a north facing sandstone escarpment commanding views over the Wollemi wilderness. An architectural competition was initiated in 2002 with a pre-selection process based upon first round 'response to the brief' submissions. From this, four teams were selected and paid to submit design proposals[ii]. The final design submissions were in July 2003 and our submission was premiated and selected to be progressed to construction, which has, however, been delayed due to Government funding problems.

The initial brief called for an 'iconic' building and 'whole of site solution' which would provide a rich interpretative experience of the diverse eucalypt communities and would acknowledge the culture of the traditional owners of the land – the Dharug and Gandagara aboriginal peoples. The brief also called for 'best practice' energy and resource utilization strategies and demanded attention to serious bushfire risk. The project offered, therefore, a beautiful opportunity to address spiritual, cultural, environmental and technical issues on a challenging site with scope for great architectural freedom. The two-stage design process encouraged a thorough exploration of a design philosophy and conceptual framework prior to embarking upon specific design solutions. The conceptual sketches and concept model were done in 2002, and the site diagram, technical section and final design submission with model were done nearly a year later in 2003.

At the outset, we visited the site several times and noted orientation, solar access, views, wind patterns, physical access, vegetation, contours, surroundings and particularly the edge escarpment with a pronounced promontory and small cave visible below. We analysed the functional brief and noted the requirements for accommodation, use, parking and we got climatic data to understand rainfall and summer and winter temperatures. We then convened a round table 'brainstorming' meeting at which we had an aboriginal cultural adviser, our landscape architect, and a leading environmental systems consultant. We had to choose from three location options within the given site, two nearer the adjoining main road and one away from the road at the edge of the escarpment. Very much guided by the question 'where would traditional inhabitants occupy the site?', we chose the remote 'edge' site because of its tranquility, solar access and views, all of which would afford greater opportunity for a truly spiritual experience.

In preparing the pre-selection submission, I was conscious of the need to present some kind of an 'architectural' vision for the centre to allow us to compete against some very well credentialed architects who would have a well known body of work to show as precedents. In Year 5 of the architecture program at the University of Newcastle, we have asked final year students undertaking their final 'thesis' projects to, at an early stage, make a concept or manifesto model which will inform their future design strategies. On a Sunday morning we were shooting images of eucalypt leaves in the forest where I lived and I decided that this is what we needed to do – to make a concept model.

Anthony Antoniades, in his book *Poetics of Architecture,* refers to studies by Daniele Pauly into the creative processes of Le Corbusier: 'Pauly has argued that these (creative) inventions were not accidental, sudden and spontaneous, but the result of a very long period of effort before he even picked up a pencil to draw. He used to store information in his memory and, as he said, use his 'human brain' as a box in which he would let 'the elements of the problem simmer".[iii]

Having gone through the analytical and the 'dreaming' processes, I downloaded a 'vision' of what the building might be. I made an A3 size box with edges that matched the site contours, filled this box with eucalypt wood shavings from my firewood shed, collected an assemblage of little bits of junk – a rusty piece of angle iron, some off-cuts of fibre cement board, a channel of aluminium, a piece of stone collected from the project site, a curved piece of wood I sprayed red, a wooden curtain ring, some tops off felt pens sprayed silver, some kebab sticks – and the model was inscribed into the site with a roof of real eucalypt leaves. I thereby captured the ideas of canopy, itinerary, meeting place with fireplace (significant to aboriginal culture), viewing 'jetty', service trench, water tanks, materiality – and how the building could be inscribed into the landscape. The concept sketches were prepared after this 'intuitive bound' – the 'picture in the mind's eye' sketch at about the size of a cigarette packet, and the rest of the sketches at the size of a matchbox. These were all included in the pre-design submission.

The principle features of the concept were a public art 'hyper-surface' sculptural roof, in the form of huge leaves, and a viewing jetty that would project over the escarpment at the level of the tops of the trees. A few days after this 'intuitive bound' with the model and the sketches, an academic colleague, having seen what I was doing, showed me the essay and sketches by Jørn Utzon, 'Platforms and Plateaux' published in Zodiac. We used quotes from Utzon in our pre-selection submission -

...the roof can be hanging above, it can be spanning across or jumping over you in one leap or in many small ones ....
.... By introducing the platform with its level the same height as the jungle top, these people had suddenly obtained a new dimension of life. [iv]

The photo images of the concept model were 'sensational' and I am sure this is what got us into the second round. A year later, having been selected as one of the four architects asked to develop the concept, the difficult issue was whether to follow the whimsical concept literally, or to interpret and transform. The 'canopy of leaves' could, on the one hand, be a piece of wonderful sculptural "hyper-surface" public art,

perhaps made from digitised real eucalyptus leaves, that would resonate with a very simple and economic building. On the other hand, the 'big leaf' idea could be a theme park joke. How much confidence could one have in a preconceived idea?

We were taught at architecture schools in the 1960's to always espouse 'reason' and to eschew flights of 'imagination' – the 'preconceived idea' was a mortal sin and one could not do it 'because I wanted to'. In teaching, I promote a both/and approach and give real value to considered use of, what I understand James Stirling referred to as, the 'f**king big idea' – I call it the 'FBI' - necessarily complemented by what I call 'LILIES' – 'lots of individual little ideas'.

[The design approach favoured] is a reversal of the conventional wisdom of the architecture schools, as [it] first formulates the solution and works back from there. ... It is an approach which is altogether at odds with the linear method of brief formulation, methodological analysis, etc., which we have heard so much of and which seems, in part at least, to have produced soulless architecture. [v]

I have been particularly interested, while teaching architecture over nearly 20 years, in the complementary interlocking relationship between a 'left brain' analytical reason-driven method and the role of 'right brain' intuitive and creative imagination.

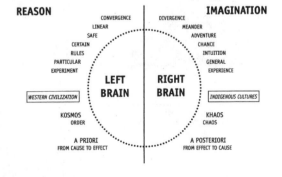

"Both/and" – reason and imagination (Lindsay Johnston, 1997) [vi]

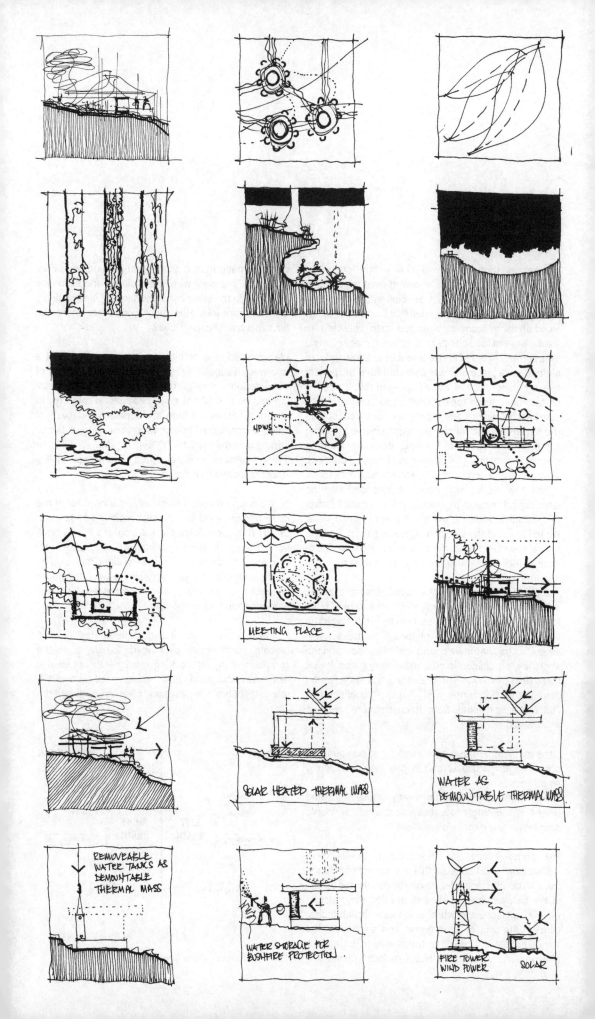

MEETING PLACE.

SOLAR HEATED THERMAL MASS

WATER AS DEMOUNTABLE THERMAL MASS

REMOVEABLE WATER TANKS AS DEMOUNTABLE THERMAL MASS

WATER STORAGE FOR BUSHFIRE PROTECTION.

FIRE TOWER WIND POWER   SOLAR

HPWS

[The design process relies on] establishing 'a vision', a picture in the mind's eye. This vision arises from a process of intuitive/ subjective thought that maps out the path for subsequent analytical/objective validation. Yet sometimes systematical analysis... sparks the complementary intuitive process. In my experience, the forces that inspire the primary generator(s) of a design, are totally unpredictable, often delicate, can vary in their nature and can come from an infinite number of directions. My position gives value to the eventual creative gesture based on intellectual gestation. The considered creative act of a line on a piece of paper which expresses the designers interpretation of a solution to the problem, or the seemingly chance movement of an element in a design model, may be the 'real truth', or certainly as good as a solution produced by a formula which may itself be flawed. I make a point of continually referring to my first sketches of The Vision , as the process evolves, to validate my intuitive and analytical refinement procedures against the first 'truth'. [vii]

During the design development process a very detailed analysis of natural levels, and how we could get enough length to provide wheelchair ramps down to the main building level, sparked – by chance(?) - another key 'move' which generated the big circle in the site layout 'diagram' and shifted the main formal pedestrian axis onto solar north, 9.5° west of magnetic north and aligned it towards the view. The 'leaf' roof was presented literally in the final competition submission with large stainless steel leafs forming a canopy over the central meeting place, supported on a 'humped' steel space frame. This has been the subject of subsequent post-competition design development, in association with public art sculptors and our structural engineer, and has yet to be finally resolved. After we had won the competition, I had to meet a committee representing the 'stakeholders' for the new facility at the site, who were not convinced about the design. We met at the site at mid-day in winter when the sun was exactly in solar north. We stood amongst the eucalypts beside the main road, and I explained -

This is where the car park will be, there will be one huge silver eucalyptus leaf at the side of the road to draw them in, they will get out of their cars and there will be another huge silver eucalyptus leaf lying on the ground which they will be drawn to – about here – now if you can follow me through the trees, we will walk directly along this axis towards the sun – the new centre will reveal itself as the cluster of huge eucalyptus leaves against the view, you won't see the building itself and the flat roof will be landscaped to replicate the natural ground around – now they will descend here, between two ponds of water, under the canopy of huge leaves into the 'meeting place' with the fireplace, and the smell of eucalypt smoke in the air and – 'pow' – there will be the view out over Wollemi wilderness. Now keep following me towards the sun – they will walk out onto the viewing jetty – out here – and that will run out on top of this rock outcrop – exactly HERE - with a glimpse back into that little cave below there and the stupendous view over the tree tops.

Lindsay Johnston grew up in Ireland and studied architecture in Scotland. After 20 years in research and practice in Ireland he emigrated to Australia and entered academic life. He has been Head of School and Dean of the Faculty of Architecture, Building and Design at the University of Newcastle, Australia. He has continued architectural practice and has been awarded for his houses and for research on and practice of environmentally sensitive strategies. He is Convener of the Architecture Foundation Australia.

i *Paraphrased from Kearney, Richard. 1988. The Wake of Imagination. Minneapolis, University of Minnesota Press, pp. 90-91.*
ii *Lindsay Johnston with David Moir Landscape Architect and other consultants; Gregory Burgess from Melbourne (RAIA Gold Medalist 2004, CAA Robert Mathew Award 1997,etc.); Innovarchi, a young Sydney practice, ex-Renzo Piano workshop, in association with aboriginal architect Dillon Kombumerri; and Nigel Bell a local specialist in 'green building'.*
iii *Antoniades, Anthony, 1990, Poetics of Architecture: Theory of Design, New York, Van Nostrand Rheinhold, p.17.*
iv *Utzon, Jørn, 1962, "Platforms and Plateaux – ideas of a Danish architect", Milan, Zodiac,No.10, pp.112-140.*
v *Quinn, Ruari, 1974, on Denis Anderson's design approach in his review of "Castlepark Village, Co. Cork", London, The Architects' Journal, 30 Oct 1974, pp.1038-1043.*
vi *Johnston, Lindsay, 1997, "Getting out of the Sheep Pen – new directions in Architectural Education", InterArch '97, paper delivered at AAC/UIA Conference, Sofia, Bulgaria, June 1997.*
vii *Johnston, Lindsay, 1994, "The Irish Mind – discourse on the design submission for the Athlone Riverside competition", Geelong, Exedra, Deakin University, Vol.5, No.2, p.11.*

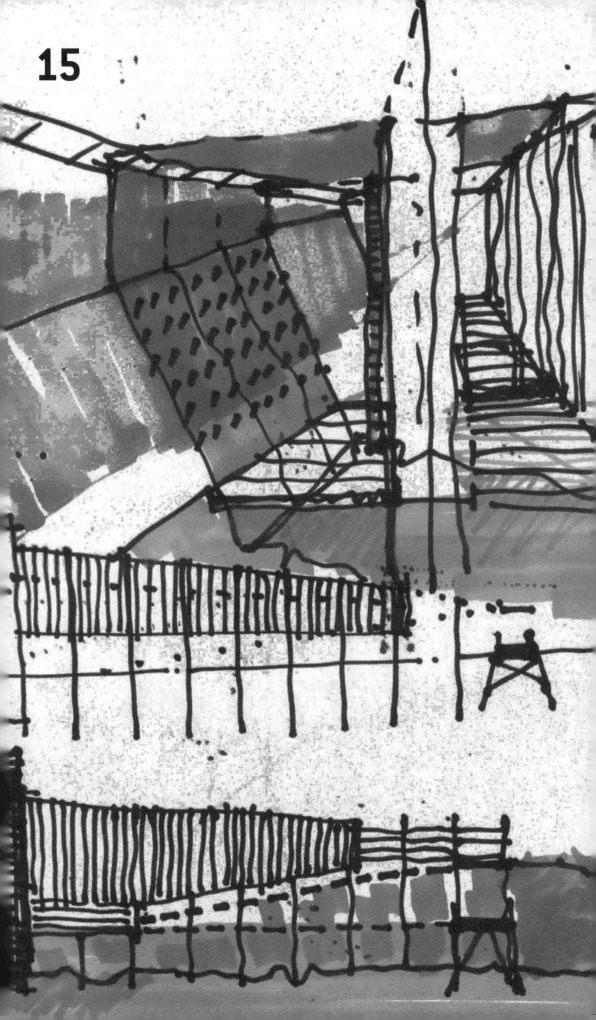

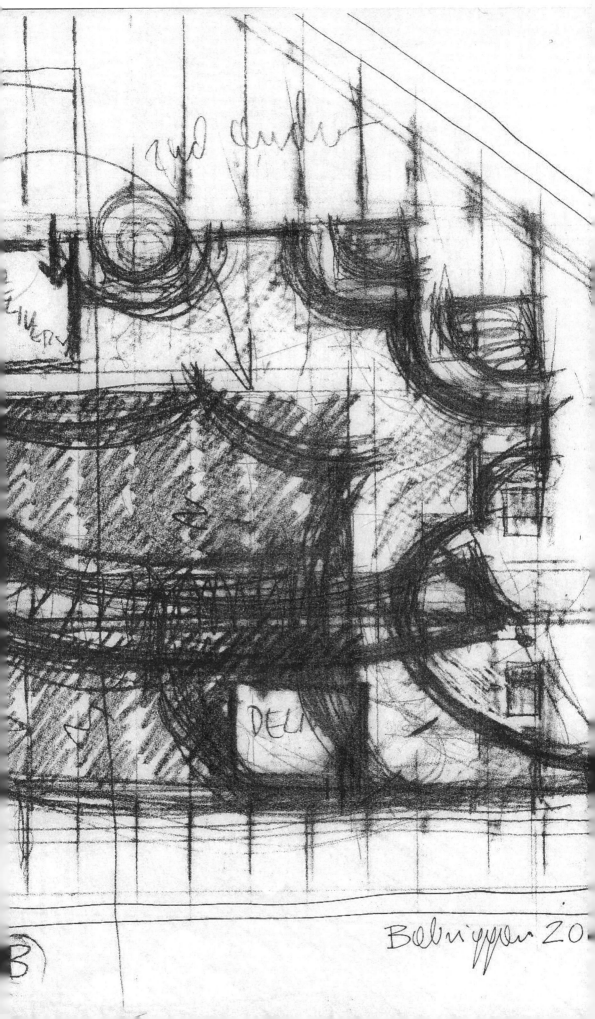

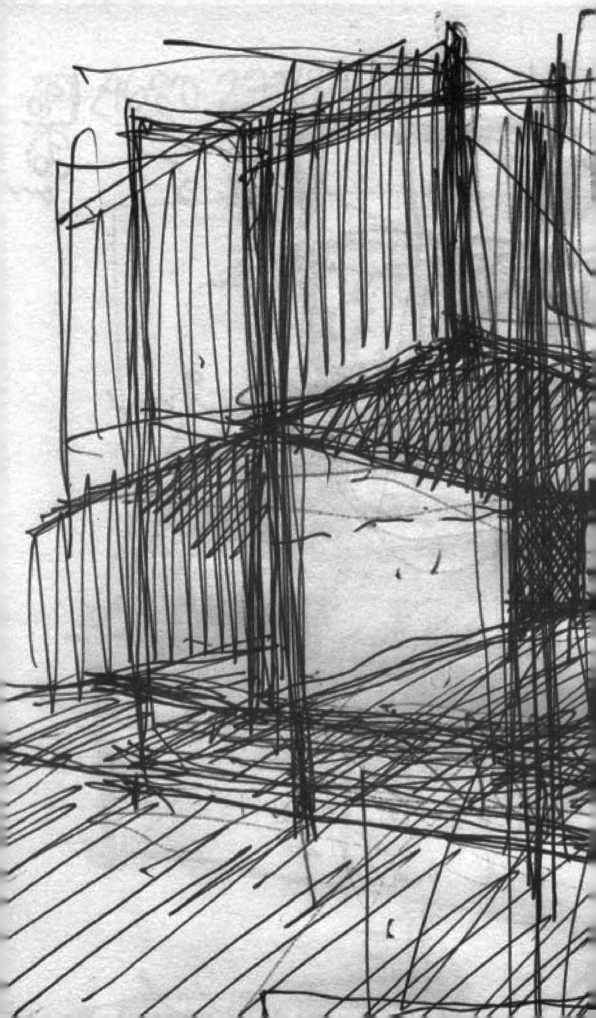

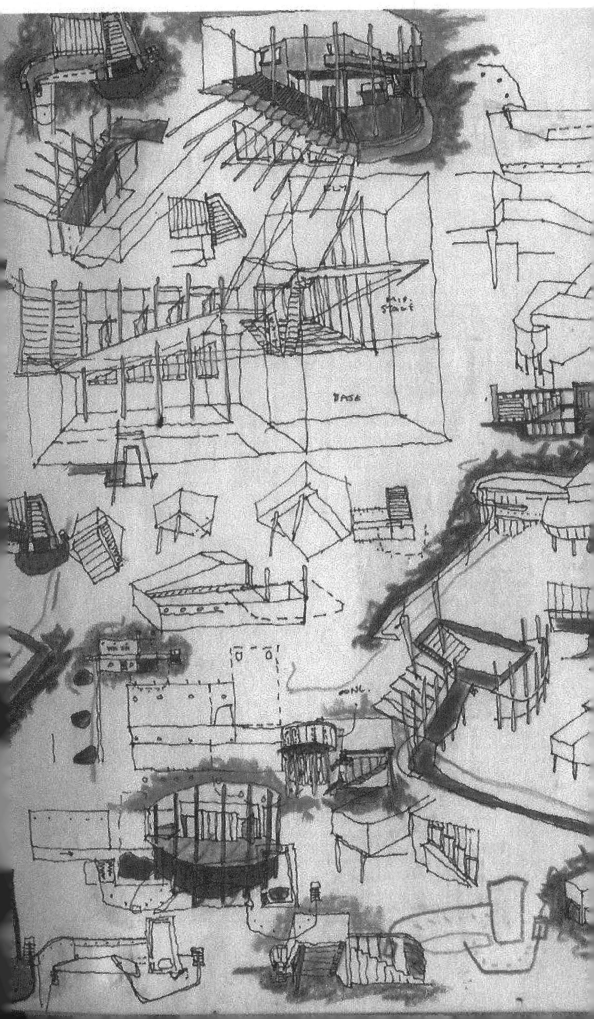

16

On models
PETER CARROLL

Models induce a proximity and nearness to a concept, the sense of secretiveness that smallness engenders. They represent an intimate and embryonic sketch in three dimensions. They capture the essential spirit of a design response, that all-important first reading that can remain as a talisman throughout the ensuing design process.

Making a model is about as close as one can get to the actual construction of a design idea. There is spontaneity, speed and penetration of design thinking when working in model form. It facilitates a freedom both for the client and the architect to avoid the predetermined and to range free and explore. It is a way of dreaming the essence of the project.

It is easy to forget the role of the model maker. The model-maker is a translator of ideas... and translation is anything but a pedestrian activity. It is a subjective process open to a wide range of interpretations. A special alchemy occurs between the architect and model-maker. It exemplifies a special working relationship. Called 'when there is something to see', model-makers are given a free hand to interpret and attempt to extrude the essence of the architect's intentions usually from scant information and under pressing deadlines. They unavoidably inject their own view of the design. In doing so, they serve as a critic bringing their own interpretation to the appearance of the design intention.

That said, I want to describe (but not necessarily explain) three models that I continuously admire and aspire towards when making models. Common to all three is the notion of a model being not only explanatory, but also generative of ideas.

The first is a part plan model of the star-shaped volume of the galleries in the *Joan Miro Foundation* in Majorca by Rafael Moneo. It is a sketch model made when a spatial idea was still fragile. A violent geometry is explored. The resultant space is a middle ground where indirect light is allowed penetrate without letting the sun's rays enter. The solid piers and horizontal baffles made of card confront an exterior yet ignore and resist it. The oblique geometries evident in the plan model capture an indescribable space, without possible definition. It is invaded by a light resulting from an unexpected chain of reflections that has nothing to do with the continuous and directed light afforded by conventional windows and rooflights.

The second is an intriguing section model of the *Cannaregio Town Square* competition entry by Peter Eisenman. This model rises out of and burrows into the ground and thinks, complicates. Its section reveals a matrix of voids. Each void is nested inside the next void like a series of Russian dolls. It is impossible to say which is the appropriate or real scale. It is also impossible to name the spaces and thus relate form to function. An interior, or fictional ground is trying to be described. Following the various thickenings of card, floors turn to become walls to become ceilings. The stability of ground is questioned. Even the notions of inside and outside are denied.

The third and final model is a paper volumetric model of part of the *Guggenheim Museum* in Bilbao by Frank Gehry. There is a tension between recognizable platonic solids among a set of spontaneous forms... something distorted away from the familiar but not so far as to cease affinity. Having the appearance of something produced rapidly, it appears unfinished and crude - the model functions like a quickly made sketch. Yet its apparent flamboyance in form disguises a very precise control in the way light is allowed fall across the convex and concave surfaces. One can imagine a slow process involving a series of physical models, where Gehry and the model-maker sit, watch and evolve each surface... an inverse of the spontaneity of impulse in Gehry's sketches.

Peter Carroll and Caomhan Murphy established A2 Architects in 2005

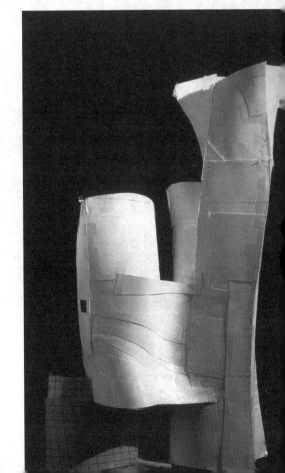

17

Models
MARTIN HENCHION

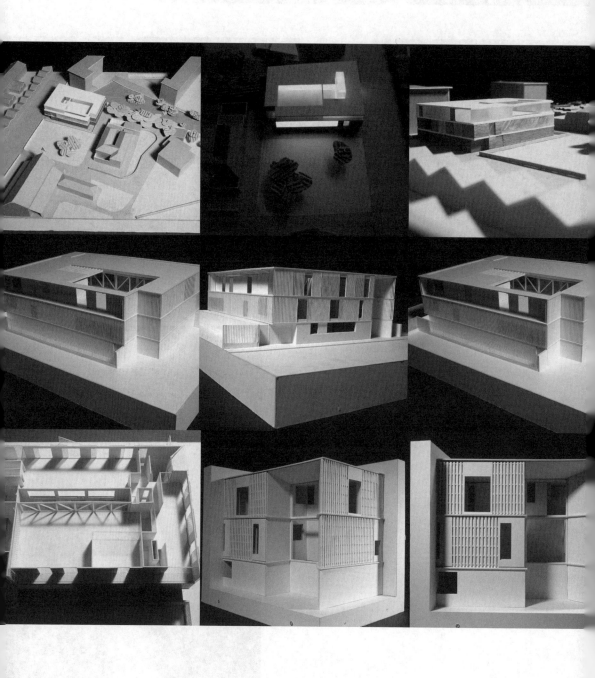

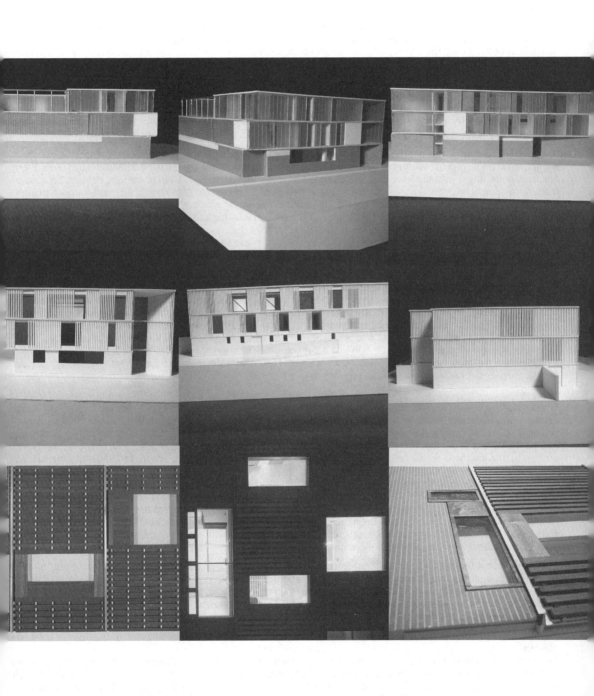

tin Henchion's early projects include an exploration of house form by means of rectangular and pyramidal shapes courtesy of Lego Ltd. is now a principal in Henchion & Reuter Architects.

18

On Details - Not Seeing The Forest
LAURA MAYES

Details

When I started making furniture I would often make a little cardboard model of the piece at the design stage, but I realised after a while that I was often disappointed with the finished piece – it was too like the model, just bigger. It had gained nothing from the change of scale, it lacked the increase in detail that changing scale requires. What are the details that go to make something satisfying in its actual manifestation?

Now, sometimes, I get lost in the details, so lost I don't what I mean by details at all – a kind of forest and trees situation. I don't know if the details are what you see when you're up close to something, or whether they are the process of the making made manifest. Can there be 'good' and 'bad' details? Are details for the 'sensitive' onlooker, the person who appreciates the challenges and elegance of solutions, or are details for everyone? Are details the expression of a solution or are they small things that can be applied to an overall form?

One possible answer: details are the result of more designing, more thought, more consideration of how the materials will act and change, in processing, in time, with use. By this way of thinking there are good details and bad ones. There are ways of putting things together that make sense and ways that don't. Some things are ugly not just because of their overall proportions and shapes but because the details of their construction have been made without thought and care. So the surface laminate laps over the substrate in the wrong way and will fall off sooner rather than later, or the wrong glue was used and is failing already, or the person working the wood didn't take account of the grain direction and there is tear-out of the grain which always catches your sweater. The details of a piece are therefore intimately connected to the way it is made. Detail is what the piece is when it's actually made.

Or perhaps details are what you see when you stand very close to something, though this depends on the size of the object to start with. Eight inches is a good distance from which to look at a jewellery box, but would be too close for a building. The details are what you see when you are a little bit too close to see the whole object. On the other hand, everything that has been made can be looked at closely, even the most nasty piece of cheap vinyl-coated mdf furniture, so everything has details in that sense. It is the eye, or hand, of the beholder which interprets what it sees, or touches, as 'good' or 'bad'. What every craftsperson hopes for is that someone will respond to what they have done – to notice, almost imperceptibly if that's possible, the subtleties, the elegance of problems solved, the choices made. They hope for someone who pays attention in a quiet way. And, of course, every craft includes some practitioners who make for the most sensitive onlookers of all – one of their own – the architects' architect, the poets' poet, the furniture-makers' furniture-maker and so on.

Process

When I start to design something I think about pairs of words - sometimes opposites, sometimes siblings - for example, inside/outside, horizontal/vertical, part/whole, plane/line, box/line, curved/straight, surface/depth, texture/colour. They are not complicated, and perhaps they are reductively Modern, an essentially futile search for separation and purity. I like to think that they help to clarify but are not the end of the story. Another pair, of course, is clarity/ambiguity. Having these words helps me move into the design – into the details - because I know that the details should work with the pairs of words, not against them. The details – the way the thing is made - reinforce the whole and the whole reinforces the details. But it's often not that clear, because the process is not a straight line, it loops and twists, goes back on itself and sometimes starts again. Often (usually, always) I don't fully know what the idea of the piece is until I start to work out how it is going to be made. Knowing how to make something clarifies what it is. It is moving between the forest and the trees, trying to see both at the same time. Sometimes even after carefully working out how the piece is to be made, still more questions come up during the process of making it, and again, I have to think about it in the context of the whole piece.

I have found that the best way to work out the details before making a piece of furniture is to draw it out full-size on a sheet of mdf. The mdf is both the drawing board and the paper but it is not going to distort or tear like paper. Sometimes making the drawing involves crawling around on top of the mdf to get to the middle of the board. I like to draw plans, sections, elevations – and the more the better. They can be right on top of each other, so I use different coloured pencil leads to (slightly) clarify what's going on. I've never managed to make a piece exactly as it's drawn though. There are always several parts that escape the set-square.

Material

I make things primarily from wood, sometimes solid, sometimes in a thin layer (though not as thin as conventional veneers) stuck to a substrate. Wood imposes a set of limitations, a set of details. Because it is in constant (albeit slow) motion to come into equilibrium with the moisture content of the surrounding environment, the design must accommodate such movement. Wood moves along the depth of the growth rings rather than in length – in practice this means it moves across the width of a plank. How much it moves depends on the cut of the timber (the orientation of the growth rings), on the species, and on the changes in humidity that it encounters. If I make something from a damp piece of wood in our quite damp workshop in Connemara and it goes to live in a centrally heated house, I know that it's going to shrink across its width. So I plan for that and avoid fixing the wood at its edges.

Unfortunately, because the growth rings of a tree are parts of a circle, and not straight lines, wood movement often manifests itself as warping. Holding a piece into a flat plane therefore becomes an issue. There is a language, a set of details that accommodates wood movement. It usually involves grooves into which the timber can expand (but out of which it will not pull if it shrinks), shadow lines that camouflage the fact that two pieces are not always flush with each other, screws that can slide in slots so that something is fixed in one direction but not in the other, and making sure that if two pieces are fixed to each other their grain direction is the same. With veneered surfaces, wood movement is no longer an issue – the substrate (a dimensionally stable manmade board) and glue overpower the thin layer of wood with the ability to move. But then the edges become not exactly a difficulty, but something that needs to be thought about – a detail in other words. Should the edgings, the pieces of wood that are often used to cover the edges of the substrate and the veneer, be there at all, or would it be appropriate to see the layers? Sometimes it can be nice to see the lines of a quality plywood. Should the edgings be applied before or after the board is veneered? Applying them before masks them on the surface, but we might want them to appear. They could be from a different timber, which would make the board look framed. And where they meet at the corners, should one run past the other – and which? – or should they be mitred at 45°?

One piece of wood looks different to another, no two look the same. Different colours, visual textures, linear patterns formed by the grain, slight curves, knots, pinholes – all these depend on where and how the tree grew and was cared for, how it was felled and planked, and then dried, stored, planed and sanded and then what finish was applied. Two planks of the same species from the same country can look completely different from each other, even two from the same tree. Perhaps there is a streak of red from an incipient fungal growth that was just in the centre of the tree. Perhaps that side faced the prevailing wind and has developed a ripple. That plank is cut with the growth rings cut perpendicular to the surface, the other with them parallel. That one has the fleck of medullary rays (part of the tree's arterial system to carry nutrients), the other has a pattern that looks like flames leaping up or wax dripping down. One has a very subtle curve, like a bow in tension, the other is going one way then the other, like long curly hair. Thinking about the pattern of the wood grain is part of making the piece of furniture. I can choose the most linear cut to emphasise the lines of the piece. Alternatively I could pick that slight curve to make a very slight supporting curve to a rail. On the back legs of a chair I can choose the grain to follow the curve – which also makes them stronger. On a tabletop I can match the pools of pattern, or offset them to create a line of movement. With veneers I can bookmatch them (opening the leaves of veneers like a book, one mirroring the other), or slip match them, or turn every second one upside-down, or put them at right angles like a parquetry floor, or arrange them randomly. It is making a composition – sometimes aiming for harmony, sometimes for contrast. Sometimes I am almost sure no one else would notice or care, and I'm annoyed with myself for taking the time. But once you have started looking it's very hard to stop until you've made a pattern of some kind, some movement or restfulness.

Details are also the extras or additions – hardware, for example. Hinges, catches, keys, locks, handles. Often they are in metal, which glints and catches the eye: they are the jewellery of a piece. They are perhaps more intricately and precisely made than the rest of the piece, and though small, they add the essential function: swinging a door to open and close it, allowing a lid to be locked and so on. Sometimes we make our own hardware – brass is surprisingly easy to work - and that means it fits the piece exactly, for example the pivot point of a hinge can be made to throw a door around a side post. But often we buy hardware too, and that means poring over catalogues, checking dimensions, checking the quality, hoping it's as good as it says it is. When it comes to handles and pulls, they can really destroy a piece if they're wrong, and they're often not very noticeable if they're right. I usually make them from wood and return to my original words about what the piece is intended to be - linear, angular, soft - to help with thinking about them, so that they reinforce the overall idea. They might be from a different wood, or might be a cut-out – a subtraction rather than an addition. In general, it seems to work better if they are smaller than I first think they should be, to bring the scale down and pull the user in. Unlike a hinge or lock, whose placement is for the most part fixed, there are usually a lot of places where a handle will function. Its placement therefore relates to the overall composition, though in itself it is a detail.

ense

I have been writing about the visual, but of course, we have other senses, and they too are involved in how we relate to an object. There is the tactile – the smoothness and silkiness of planed wood, finished with a little oil, or the exposed grain of scrubbed oak. There is a place that just fits your finger to open a door, inviting you to open it. The size of a handle or pull influences the way the door will be opened – delicately, gingerly, robustly. For that one you must turn your hand vertically, or the other horizontally, for that one you need to lower your head, while for another you can grab and pull. When you sit on a chair, your hand can idly caress the gentle curve on the front of the arm or under the front of the seat. A traditional drawer has wooden sides and fits into a wooden pocket. The sound of wood against wood on a well-fitted drawer or the click of a door finding its resting place are quiet pleasures.

Once you've started to compile a language of details, a repertoire, a compendium, you start an anti-list – a list of pet-hates, a snobbish disdain for certain details. I don't like mitred joints, in fact I don't like 45° at all. It is too unhierarchical. I like precedence given to one thing over another, verticals over horizontals or vice versa. I don't like two-toned wood choices, especially with a high contrast, walnut and maple for example. I'm not sure if I like through joints – exposed joints – apart from dovetails. And with dovetails, I like the pins to be skinny. As you can see, it is easy to slip into meaningless peeves. I don't like sprayed on lacquer finishes, though I know they have to be used in high-traffic situations or where nobody is really going to care. I prefer planed surfaces over sanded ones. The rationale is that a plane cuts the fibres cleanly while sanding tears at them with progressively finer grits, and a cut surface reflects the light and feels smoother than a sanded surface ever will. But in truth it could purely be that I know planing is more difficult than sanding and I appreciate the workmanship that planing implies.

I also like the small set-backs and shadowlines that wood impose. The blankness of construction that conventionally veneered panels allow has a scalelessness that disturbs me. They remind me of my own disappointment with the first pieces of furniture I made – that they looked like small cardboard models blown up to whatever size. They lacked the increasing level of detail that an increase in the scale should bring, like a digital image that gets increased without meaning until large pixels fill the screen. It is a dream of filmmakers, one that Charles and Ray Eames realised in the film Powers of Ten: the long shot that goes from outer space down towards the earth, towards a certain country, then city, building or place, room, person, up close to that person, into their skin, into their veins, in and in to the nucleus of a carbon atom – there is no such thing as detail, just a changing perspective. For me, with my limited powers of space travel and microscopic vision, I try to see the forest and trees and branches and leaves and veins, to know that they are intimately related, that they are the same thing, and to not get lost in one at the expense of the others.

Laura Mays works as a furniture designer and maker in the partnership Yaffe Mays in northwest county Galway and teaches at the Furniture College in Letterfrack.

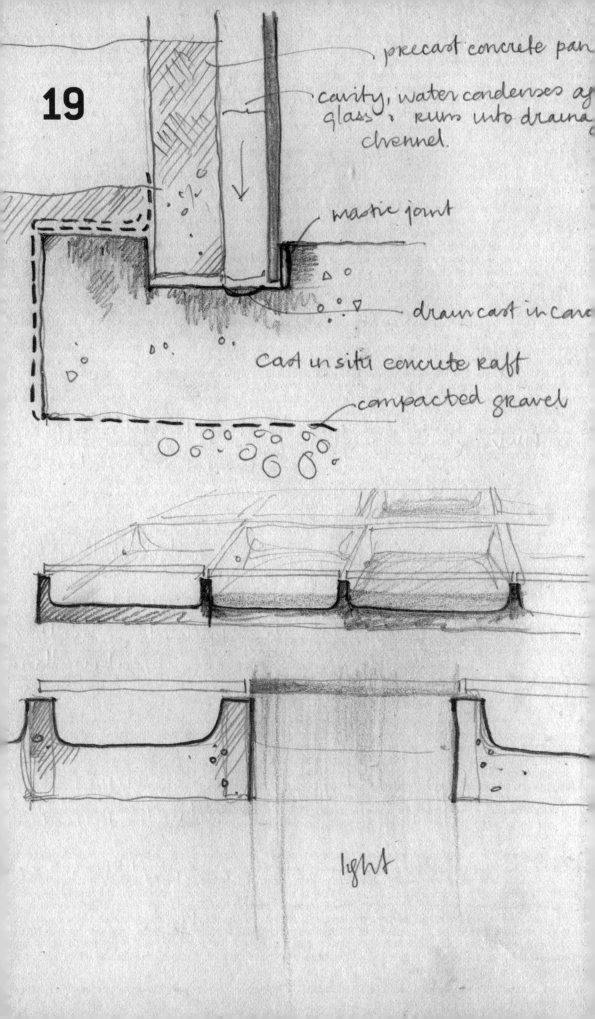

19

precast concrete pan

cavity, water condenses ag
glass, runs into draina
channel.

mastic joint

drain cast in cond

cast in situ concrete raft

compacted gravel

light

BLOCKING VEILING

2ND METHOD Block...
Sew Back seam.
Hole in top Gather
Block on whimsey ske...
and then size.

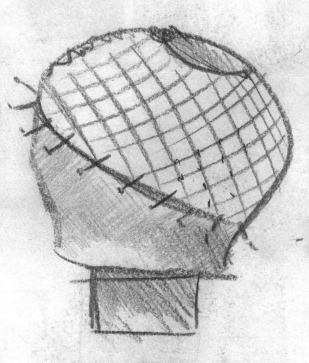

— whimsey

Gather en
and wind
around
stitch

...ound whumsey and gather end
...zether knoting

... at bottom.

...centre wind
stitch

...m working repeat o size.

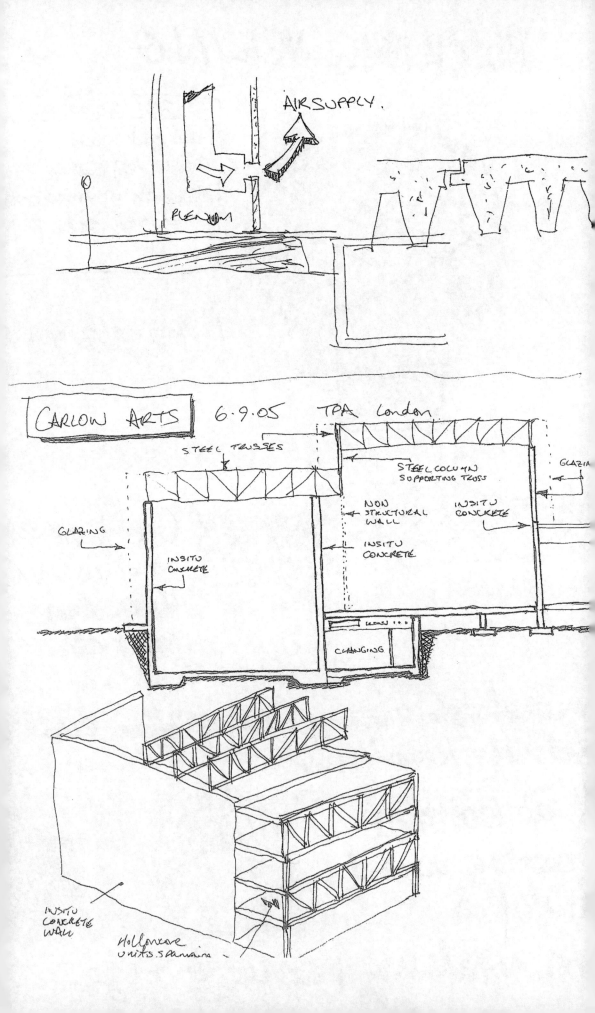

AIR SUPPLY.

PLENUM

CARLOW ARTS   6·9·05   TPA London

STEEL TRUSSES

GLAZIN

STEEL COLUMN
SUPPORTING TRUSS

NON
STRUCTURAL
WALL

INSITU
CONCRETE

GLAZING

INSITU
CONCRETE

INSITU
CONCRETE

CHANGING

INSITU
CONCRETE
WALL

Hollowcore
units spanning

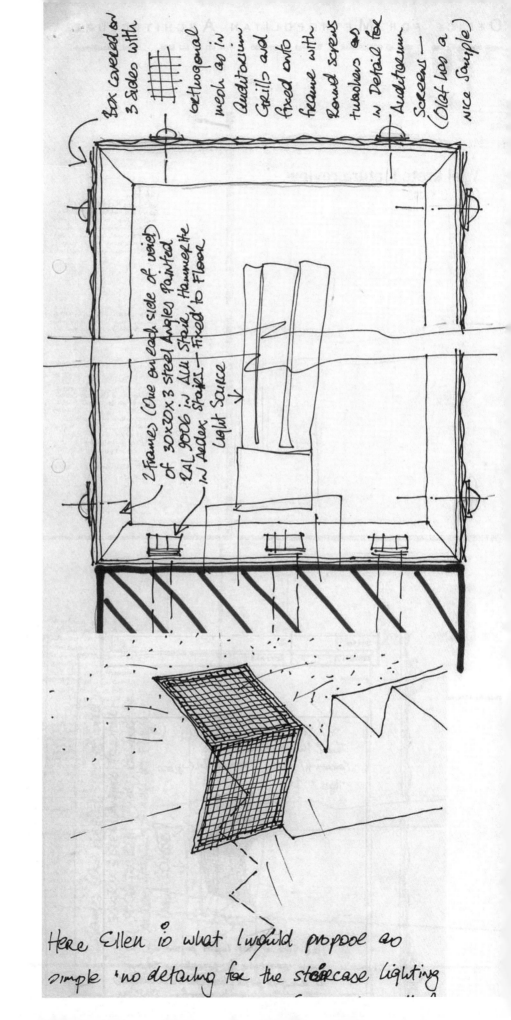

Box covered on 3 sides with orthogonal mesh as in Auditorium Grills and fixed onto frame with Round screws turnbuckles as in Detail for Auditorium Screens — (Olaf has a nice Sample)

2 Frames (One on each side of unit) of 30x30x3 steel Angles Painted RAL 9006 in Alu Stove Hammer fix in peder Straps — fixed to Floor

Light Source ↓

Here Ellen is what I would propose as simple · no detailing for the staircase lighting

20

Wiel arets lecture review
ORLA O'KANE

FO(A)RM
Wiel Arets Architects - Bettina K.
Tea/coffee set for Alessi "Tea
and Coffee Towers" 4 piece
+ TRAY. Reduction of the
functional components to
substraction rather than
additions. Cut out from solid.

Red + clear glass objects.
Traditional sets: a skyline
on a table. Now solid

volumes of same size.

TRANSPORT PICTOGRAMS
Coloured farther corres-
ponding to plan's route
lines. Movie Museum
Amsterdam - curved
mirrored surfaces - trippy
kaleidoscopic effect.
Big window over city
in cinema auditorium
- cool!
E.TH Science City
Zurich. Streets are our

dimensioned. Instead of
minimising the streets a
layer of tarmac - up to site
border - to contain all
future building. On the
tarmac - graphics. Draw
everything on the
ground - signs/icons
(oversized) etc. Perforation
pattern came from
"schmoozing".
TWO GREENHOUSES

Hen house is
part of the
house, as in
an art coll-
ection. 3
interlocking
circulation routes.
Collection of space w/
variety of functions.
HEDGE HOUSE is its name.

The gardener pitched the
hedge to match the roof
on the house.
Neeko's Hall Maastricht...?
Jellyfish house - focus
on upper levels and
big ideas about routes
and circulation - central
theme in general?

Mallorca? Or Marbella?
Pool on the Roof. The

stairs
are
both
steep
and
also
shallow - working to
differentiate the
movement - speed! It
can be entered at all
levels. Interlocking.
STYLE SUITE MAASTRICHT
All required programme
within a double wall.
For the
purpose of
visibility I
think - a
diagonal cut
through
the plan.
EUROPOL DENHAAG
Public realm expressed
by opening up the
ground floor. Skin
says "yes this is a
safe building"

University Library Utrecht
...Orange plan block
outline on a black and
white photo - Nice!
Contemporary library
= 2 conflicts in concept.

Role of
book
changed.
Digital
Media
Sound!
Opaque clouds = the
book storage spaces.
Near the glass reading
rooms - open/free.
Display of books N.B.
Not a temple. An
interchange for flow
movement information.
'Huge' reception - Soto
calm people down on
entering.
AMSTERDAM ART
METROPOLE

Cinema w/window
overlooking city -
a leitmotif?

Orla O'Kane is a 5th year student of architecture but hopes to expand into different areas of design and work with a variety of other creative disciplines. She plays the viola and plans to study shoe-design, seeing it as a logical progression from her current studies.

21

AAI History
ELLEN ROWLEY

This is the first of a two-part historical review of the AAI. In the following piece Ellen Rowley presents the reader with a description of the Association's role in terms of architectural culture in post-war Ireland. This section draws on the polemics of the AAI's annual publication, the Green Book (1945-75), as a primary source and in so doing, presents a long-forgotten and neglected journal to a new generation.

The post-war life and legacy of a forgotten journal...
The public will no longer speak of us in whispers as those arty guys who had some remote connection with the adornment of ecclesiastical buildings in the middle ages...we have come to life and are actually stepping down off our lofty spires to squat on their own doorsteps. After all! There is no earthly reason why the man in the street should not be conscious of the street architecture.[i]
(Dermot O'Toole, AAI President's 'Inaugural Address', 1943 - 44)

Like the nature of the medium it presents and the identity of the nation it represents, the Architectural Association of Ireland has inevitably changed and reshaped itself over the course of its history. Almost on a decade-by-decade basis there has been a decipherable shift in priority. Such continual metamorphosis, managed and informed by its youthful and ever-transient committee, has sustained an *avant-garde* tendency in terms of its activity content. And while the fashion-forming and taste-bending which has explicitly informed AAI activity since the mid-1990's must be congratulated, the Association's perpetual vibrancy is only assured through continuous self-examination.

This review represents the preliminary stage in a research project that seeks to understand and contextualise Irish architecture from the late 1940s until the early 1990s. The AAI's central placement in relation to the discourse of Irish architecture in the post-war period has naturally led to an examination of its recent history. Its shifting identity as an academic, culturally inclined body has always differentiated itself from the Royal Institute of Architects of Ireland, (RIAI) allying itself more closely to student endeavour and aspiration. But instead of glibly accepting such an image, we must explore its' activities over time to more clearly ascertain its role within the society of Irish architecture.

The first stage in this process must constitute a reading of its journal, the *Green Book*. Taking an overview of this long-neglected source from c.1950 until its end in the mid 1970s, there emerges a perceptible pattern in both critical thinking and approaches to architecture. A wealth of opinion resides in each of the Presidents' addresses which, significantly take the form of themed musings on the state of Ireland's architectural world. There is a discernable lack of intellectual arrogance in the addresses, most probably resulting from the fact that these 'essays' are forms of oral histories which have been transcribed, spell-checked and tidied up a little. Due to this, I suggest, they may inadvertently guide us to a more 'truthful' definition of architectural culture at a given time.

The *Green Book* enables us to situate the AAI upon its horizon, both historically and culturally. We can then begin to recognise that the current approach to the role of 'keeper-of-the-architectural-culture-of-Ireland,' is not infallible. To acknowledge exemplary contemporary practice at home primarily through the diagnosis/prophecy of a foreign critic (i.e. *New Irish Architecture* (NIA) awards), and to provide 'show and tell' monologues by renowned international forces (i.e. AAI lectures), is not how the Association has always sought to define itself...

We must endeavour, then, to make available for the rising generation a sound training which will strengthen its sense of duty and to make that sense an abiding one.[ii]
(A E Williams, AAI President's 'Inaugural Address', 1942-43)

Originally founded for educational purposes, we are reminded of the AAI's Constitutional dictum: 'The objects of the Association shall be: to promote and afford facilities for the study of Architecture and the Allied Sciences and Arts and to provide a medium of friendly communication between members and others interested in the progress of Architecture. Whilst today it continues to cite this dual-aim of providing education and initiating discourse, the Association has in essence been redirecting itself since the successful emergence of formalised architectural education, firstly at the National University and then at the Technical College in Bolton street.[iii]

The change in tone from the predominantly educational to the more discursive is generally considered to have occurred during the 1930s and with this shift, as Brian O'Connell asserts, the AAI had become '...a learned society, whose membership and executive were largely graduate: its interest became the essence and application of architecture.'[iv] However a reading of the AAI post-War annuals, especially the Presidents' inaugural addresses therein, reveals an ongoing questioning of the Association's raison d'etre in the 1940s; a nervous energy, emphatic in tone, underlies the polemic of the period whence the traditional apprentice and office-based learning was being undermined by these newly founded collegiate courses. J P Alcock's 1945 Presidential address describes the AAI's former role as, '...providing the embryo

GREEN
BOOK
1967-1968

JOURNAL OF THE ARCHITECTURAL ASSOCIATION OF IRELAND

Architect with a wide acquaintance of professional colleagues, by holding classes in planning and design where young minds enjoyed the healthy stimulus of competition, by placing an adequate library at the service of the student and by fostering an atmosphere of liberal study uncoloured by a too great emphasis on the purely utilitarian.'[v]   He goes on to propose a new purpose for the Association: 'The education of an Architect does not end with his student days. It continues in the school of experience and is greatly aided by the discussions and the pooling of knowledge which a society such as ours encourages...we must take a still broader view, and... in this broader view we shall see that architectural education should not be confined to Architects and students...' [vi]

It is clear at this point that the Association both needed and sought to redeem itself in terms of its principal activities and Alcock's proposal, and in its consideration of the *non-architect*, evidently makes a step towards such 'redemption'; his proposition is still didactically-inclined, but importantly it signals inclusiveness. Indeed, within a few years of his appeal we see the Association amending its Constitution so as to accommodate the hoped-for inclusion of the *'layman'.*[vii]   Soon the act of informing the public about architecture becomes the AAI's primary *theoretical* aspiration. And for the following fifty or so years this aim appears at the forefront of the Association's discourse.

Presidents and award-assessors alike repeatedly warn us against the danger of elitism to Irish architectural development. From Desmond FitzGerald's address in 1948 we learn that 'fashionable foibles and voguish whimseys' may only be overcome through inclusion of and deference to the public.[viii] He refers to 'a process of inbreeding' which diseases architecture and results in 'an exotic bloom so remote from reality and the aspirations of the period as to be of interest only to those of a precious outlook and breeding.'[ix] FitzGerald's caution is markedly echoed by Sam Stephenson in 1997, when in the latter's role as assessor of the *New Irish Architecture* awards he comments, 'The intention to 'inform the public of new directions in architecture' might be helped by having more non-architects on the jury, thus minimising the danger of architectural gamesmanship between ourselves in favouring buildings that please other architects...' [x]

It would seem that the Association perceived its changing role from this time, the 1940s, as being that of evangelist rather than educationalist - there is an inherent reciprocal nature underlying architecture, between its production and reception, and so the AAI must draw attention to this reciprocity! Again FitzGerald's words enforce the point: '...Architecture thrives when it is accepted as a part of general culture, and when it is the subject of criticism of an interested public.'[xi]   And he goes on to describe how the Association must become a national milieu for critics and architects alike, where such interest can breed and stimulate architectural development.[xii] A pedantic tenor emanates from the pages of the yearbooks as each president attempts to (re)assert both the Association's national-societal purpose and architecture's universal-humanist responsibility; Dermot O'Toole maintains in 1943 that, 'The physical picture of a country is the hall-mark of its culture', while J Morgan states, 'It is my belief that our Association in a very limited way could help in the long arduous task of contributing towards a more cultured people. It will not occur in our lifetime but, somehow, future generations must be imbued with these instincts.' [xiii]

Such pedantry at play is what we have come to expect from architectural discourse during this period and stems from the typically prescriptive tendencies of the profession at the time; that architecture may cure society's (Post-Emergency) ills was by now an accepted stance. Interestingly the ongoing petition from the AAI *Green Book* seems not to be for the salvation of the Irishman's body or indeed his soul, but rather of his cultural self. The mantra states that good architecture cultivates a people while that people cultivate good architecture – but, does this exchange produce 'a more cultured people'? And importantly, does such a dialogue equate to a healthy architectural culture?

It is disappointing to see how few public buildings, apart from hospitals, are being erected in the city. In other countries, rich business men and wealthy industrialists vie in presenting swimming pools, libraries and so forth to their cities. Here those people buy racehorses.
(C Aliaga Kelly, AAI President's 'Inaugural Address', 1951- 52.)[xiv]

It is precisely the AAI's endeavour to establish a culture-of-architecture that this paper seeks to describe and explore. To approach an understanding of the term, we must accept that it cannot be abstractly defined because its meaning is never constant. In this way then we conclude that 'cultural' (in the Irish context) through the 1940s was by necessity defined by questions of the national; during the 1950s it becomes wholly informed by emigration, and the 1960s' definition is rooted in economic expansion, and so on, through contemporary Irish history. While architectural production is commonly read as an expression of a culture – Fintan O'Toole's comment in the AAI award scheme of 1993 that, 'Good architecture has a great deal to do with a healthy intersection between a culture and an economy', is representative of this accepted reading – we are interested in the specific understanding of the culture within or of architecture. Although reductive, a dictionary definition can be useful in highlighting key aspects of this complex term; hence *culture* denotes 'taste, intellectual development at a time or place, cultivation, refinement'.[xv] Traditionally it is the characteristic which separates humans from animals, the civilized from the primitive. In architectural terms we are reminded of Nikolaus Pevsner's notorious differentiation between examples of architecture (the civilized) and buildings (the primitive). Today, like many of modernity's determinist groupings, Pevsner's boundary has become blurred and easily dismissed, and accordingly the AAI has continuously sought to present Irish architecture - vernacular, historical, classical or otherwise - as a whole. However, the Association does culturally discriminate in the direction of the ubiquitous 'fat-cat' developer, or even the down-trodden planner. As Shane O'Toole explains, Irish architecture, through the AAI generally but the *New Irish Architecture* awards in this particular instance, must '...ensure its perception as being independent from the commercial support and influence of the construction industry.' [xvi]

The culture of architecture then, as nurtured by the AAI, is increasingly predicated on an intellectual, a-commercial refinement. While in reality architectural production can never forget the commercial, the culture of architecture focuses on questions of client need, design/ technical prowess, environment/ context, user response/ reception and significantly, the critical summation of these constituents. The most recent manifestation, and inducement, of these principles is the Association's award scheme. Now in its twenty-first year, the scheme, like the Association which presents it, has undergone changes and shifts in emphasis while remaining singular in its critical review of Ireland's annual architectural tendencies. [xvii] Because the awards are all about contemporary architecture, there is a lack of objectivity for which retrospective judgement allows. In negative terms buildings have not yet had the chance to perform; conversely, the contemporary nature of the selected architecture each year encourages fledgling powers to emerge earlier and thus develop more 'roundly' over time. But either way, in my opinion, New Irish Architecture signals an addiction to a historicist, here-and-now narrative of Irish culture where all building and especially the exemplary, appears to be guided by a national (technological) zeitgeist.

While the awards are undoubtedly contemporary-architecture-for-contemporary-architects, this does not negate their validity. The process attempts to be as inclusive and comprehensive as possible and must be congratulated particularly in light of the limited budget.[xviii] Essentially the scheme's public face takes the form of the aforementioned publication and then an exhibition (a harem of A1 boards which journey on a questionable national jaunt), and in this respect it attempts to fulfil its aim as stated in 1986, '...to bring the best work of Irish architects to the attention of the public... inform of emerging directions in contemporary architecture and promote recognition of a new generation of architects.'[ixx] The entire enterprise continues to be dependent upon the energy-levels of the 'next generation', represented by a select group of individuals; their voluntary status, and to a lesser extent their youth, suggest that the cultural activity surrounding architectural production is deemed of little value within Irish society. Orna Hanly's statement in 1987 that the, '...traditional role of the AAI has been in the facilitation and promotion of architectural thought in this country'[xx] reinforces this image of the AAI as something of a lone Quixotic figure in Ireland's culturally-barren built environment. And ten years later, as our infamous tiger growled in the background, Shelley McNamara reinforces the Association's singular cultural role when she asserts, 'I am convinced that good work needs this culture or milieu in order to survive and develop, and the AAI Awards and events programme is critical to this development.'[xxi] Naturally Irish architecture becomes defensive when confronted with perceived disinterest. And yet, the reality of the AAI's ongoing financial challenge and lack of suitable home contradicts both last year's welcome arrival of a national architectural foundation, and indeed the presence and recent success of Ireland at the international architectural 'playground', the Venice Biennale.[xxii] Are things turning around? Certainly the relatively recent creation of the position of 'Architecture Specialist Consultant', on to the State's cultural body, the Arts Council, presupposes a newfound centrality for architecture-as- culture in the twenty first century. [xxiii]

...I believe that part of the withdrawal of Architecture from the layman (or vice versa) was due to the mystifying intellectualisation of the Art of Architecture Aesthetes like Ruskin. (James O'Toole, AAI President's "Inaugural Address", 1969-70)[xxiv]

It is important to note at this point that the NIA awards and their accompanying publication were born partly out of the need to fill a void left by the demise of the aforementioned Association's annual (or often bi/tri-annual), the Green Book. Having represented the Association in the form of the President's address, the annual report on events, competition briefs/ guidelines and then an article or two of mixed approach and quality, the Green Book is now maintained as a statistics-based newsletter, something of a necessary afterthought, at the back of New Irish Architecture.[xxv] It last appeared as an independent journal, albeit in summarised form, in 1975 whence three consecutive Presidents rather typically chastise various aspects of architectural production in Ireland. The first, Peter Ferguson aims his criticism at Governmental negligence in terms of master-planning and competitions, followed by Brian O'Connell's angst at the apparent flooding of 'foreign advisers' and 'experts' into the world of Irish architecture and building.[xxvi] Add an article about the practice of West Coast American architect Craig Ellwood, and the quietly iconic publication ends with the President from 1974-75, Rev Ronan Geary SJ, discussing the possibility of Irish Church design adopting Robert Venturi's philosophy and Las Vegas' forms! Just a quick glance at a single, random (albeit the last), Green Book infers the richness and contemporaneity of the journal's content generally.

Commonly the Presidents' addresses, and indeed most secondary articles in the Green Book, refrain from discussing specific buildings or practices, preferring to refer to generic architectural examples. For instance, during the early 1960s there seems to be a preoccupation with 'the church' and modern design, while the latter half of that decade tends to concentrate upon 'the city' and issues of conservation.[xvii] Does this more abstracted discourse denote the hoped-for 'cultural'-superiority or bias of the Green Book? Certainly in the 1950s- 60s, the AAI left the more bricks-n-mortar analysis of Ireland's architectural development to such 'renegade' publications as Architectural Survey.[xxviii] Although all site visits and the occasional lecture dealt with a specific contemporary or recent Irish building, it would seem that until the onset of the award scheme in 1986, whose publications continue to derive all their critical content from particular buildings, the AAI sought to be somewhat abstruse in its criticism of contemporary Irish architecture.

The combined effects of this and the historical and ongoing dearth of open competitions in this country, has led to the traditional opinion of Irish architecture as having an impoverished culture and an absence of critical discourse. Architectural historian Edward McParland, in the role of non-architect assessor for the NIA awards in 1998, stated: 'It has long been acknowledged that one of the handicaps under which the art of contemporary architecture suffers is the lack of serious criticism. The 1996 report Developing a Government Policy on Architecture rightly complained (2.5.3) that 'Public debate on architectural matters is virtually non-existent, yet debate and criticism is especially important and must be encouraged by every means...'[xxix]

But critical reticence may be a national rather than a genre-specific phenomenon. Indeed, even the more developed, critically-speaking, discipline of literary studies in Ireland decries the perceived Irish suspicion of criticism. At a recent Irish Studies conference Joe Cleary asked, 'Where is our Said, Kristeva, our Luckas? Ours is a text-based criticism which has nothing to do with Irish popular culture and stems from the middle class... the gap between Joe Public and Irish Criticism is growing.'xxx Essentially Cleary, the literary scholar, points out that there is no shortage of important writers/artists/architects, but he ponders upon the existence of our cultural theorists and thinkers. Are we all afraid of 'proper' criticism? Apparently so, according to the established architect and architectural commentator, Sean O'Laoire when he asserts in 1993 that, 'Ireland is at once blessed and bedevilled by the smallness and homogeneity of its population. In a small community, the maintenance of a critical debate is often hindered by our fondness for each other and our fear of giving offence'xxxi Such bemoaning certainly highlights a national paucity of criticism, stemming most pointedly from insularity.

Another reason for this paucity may stem from the mutual exclusivity of theory and building. Following a minor building boom the President, C Aliaga Kelly, comments in the *Green Book* of 1951 that there appeared to be a '...lack of burning zeal in theory and practice'. He goes on to describe the situation whereby, 'Paradoxical as it may be, architects may have been too busy to think deeply. When the contractor and client are ringing up all day for 'the plans', one feels one cannot decide to analyse the exact shape which a particular window should be...'xxxii Kelly supposes that theorising, can only occur in the space of architectural inactivity. He wonders why there are no Irish architects writing books, but perhaps reveals the true spirit of his time when he states, 'It is a sad thought that the best book so far published on Dublin and its architecture is published in England...' xxxiii

A reading of the *Green Books* reveals an Association which is the scene of a constantly shifting debate. This is perhaps most evident in the 1950s. The decade is generally considered as Ireland's bleak period, not least when it comes to the state of architectural development therein. However, it yields a surprisingly lively and creative, if not zany, crop of *Green Books* which merits brief elaboration here. Amidst great moments of lucidity, (one key example being Luan Cuffe's excellent photo story from 1957) the direction and tone of the Association, as expressed via the *Green Books*, seems at times confused and bizarre. The 1954 President, Sydney Maskell reckons that the AAI should reconsider the seriousness of its role as the 'purveyor' of the culture of Irish Architecture, 'And so I put it to you that the Association is drifting not by design, but by force of present day tendencies, from a cultural and academic background to a lighter and, dare I say, a more entertaining future'. Meanwhile his successor in 1955 Frank Purcell reasserts the Association's educational-bias: '...the emphasis in our activities has in the last half century shifted away from the purely educational. It is perhaps time to direct once more our efforts towards educational work... It is however essential if we are to fulfil our objects that we make every effort to educate public taste.'xxxiv

As well as accomodating split personalities on an annual basis, the *Green Books* at this juncture provided space for comic and dramatic interludes. The student competition brief from 1951-52 for a 'School in County Kill' is described to the unfortunate students at the time as follows: 'A small religious community, fleeing from persecution in Central Europe, has settled in Ireland, intending to establish a Boarding School for boys. The principal, Rev. Fr. Dubrovnik, has come to you, a leading young Irish architect, as one most likely to sympathise with his ideas and provide what he requires... He has an eye worthy of a medieval abbot... [When quizzed about finances he answers]... "Money? – God is good," says Fr. Dubrovnik... Fr. Dubrovnik has this in mind as a possible site for an open-air theatre – a project which should not be discouraged at this stage. Sooner or later he will grow to understand the Irish climate.'xxxv One suspects that the comedy is satirical and just requires a more lateral analysis in terms of its validity as a resource for contemporary Irish architectural history. An hilarious and poignant example from 1952 recounts the proceedings of an architectural study group who are advising on a potential design for Leinster House: "In the treatment of the site special consideration has been given to the most modern interpretation of spatial relationships. Not only is the exterior, through the medium of a plate glass screen wall, designed to flow into the interior, but, and this we regard as a significant advance, the interior is designed to flow into the exterior." xxxvi

From this skittish account one may assume that an element of intellectual Tom Wolfe-like fatigue, induced by Modernist-speak, is at play! But if such examples seem irreverent to our more consciously cultural motivations today, we have only to remember that just a few years later in 1964, this same Association is addressed by the iconic Buckminster Fuller, followed in 1965 by the emerging figure of James Stirling. xxxvii

It can be imagined of no heroine in fiction that she ill spent her youth among the Architects.
Sacheverall Sitwell xxxviii

In temporary conclusion then, the *Green Book*, just like the Association it represents and the medium it presents, is never constant in its polemic. It does however correspond to a sincere and unceasing pursuit of an expression of Ireland's culture of architecture. The words of Niall Montgomery from 1956 reveal the oft-uncanny (and not *un-heimlich*) that might emerge from the Architectural Association of Ireland at any given time in its Post-War history:

Replan for what we have, but build up high, wide and handsome, noble dwellings shining in the light and air of city parks, balance them with terraces, churches, schools. Make the city, between the canals, inaccessible to private motor cars and... don't exile decent Dublin men to the far foreign fields of Dundrum and Ballygall. xxxix

To be continued...

Ellen Rowley is a lecturer in the Department of History of Art + Architecture, Trinity College Dublin. She teaches courses on Approaches to Architectural History + Criticism, and Art + Society. Her M.Phil thesis at Cambridge School of Architecture was on Austrian-born but New York-based architect-artist, Frederick Kiesler (1890 - 1965) and Surrealist Architecture; currently she is researching a doctorate on the subject of Post-War Irish Architecture.

i Taken from Green Book, (AAI annual, Dublin, 1943-44), p.27.

ii Taken from Green Book, (1942-43), p.31.

iii For a concise well-written history of the AAI see: Brian O'Connell, "A History of the Architectural Association of Ireland", in Green Book, (1971-75). This history was described in the annual report as follows: "The main highlight of the 1973-74 series of events was the tracing of the Architectural Association of Ireland's history and purpose by Brian O'Connell", (then President). For more on the inception of the Association see: "The Proposed Dublin Architectural Association" in The Irish Builder and Engineer, (Nov. 1st 1896, Vol. XXXVIII, No. 885), p. 223; "The Architectural Association of Ireland" in The Irish Builder, (Nov 15th 1896, Vol. XXXVIII, No. 886), p.233; "The Artistic, Literary, and Scientific Institutions of Dublin. Part V – The Architectural Association of Ireland" in The Irish Builder, (July 3 1915), p.298-300. For the earlier C20 role and history of AAI, and the emergence of Third Level architectural education, see: Sean Rothery, Ireland and the New Architecture, (Lilliput Press, Dublin 1991), p.60-2, p.103, p.131-137. Finally, Shane O'Toole compiled a brief history after O'Connell's (above) which accompanies the AAI's Constitution and Rules, see John O'Regan (ed.), New Irish Architecture, (AAI award scheme annual, No.1, 1986), p.39.

iv O'Connell, Green Book, (1971-75) p 21-22; O'Connell explains that in 1930, the Association underwent "...a subtle change in its role" so as to become "...a platform and forum of architectural opinion".

v J P Alcock, President's "Inaugural Address", Green Book, (1944-45) p.29. Here Alcock simply describes the reasons for the AAI's involvement in architectural training and education. The issue of education dominates the committee meeting discussions from 1944-45-46 and a specific education sub-committee appears to have been created. For an example of such discussion see Architectural Association of Ireland Minute Book 1944, proceedings of meeting from 21st March 1944: "Miss Butler proposed 'that when considering the question of defining "approved schools" the RIAI should confine such approval to a University School in order that Architectural Education may be higher education comparable with that for the other professions'... Mr Fitzgerald then put forward the proposal 'that this Committee supports the view of the RIAI that the most satisfactory method of receiving architectural Education is by a course of study at an approved university leading to an architectural degree.'"

vi Alcock, "Inaugural Address" in Green Book (1944-45), p.30.

vii The Constitution was amended in 1948 by Messrs Barry, Butler, Le Clerc and Alcock and passed unanimously on June 9th 1948. The significant change in terms of this paper is as follows: "Laymen and women are now eligible to join the Association but have no voting powers", Green Book, (1949-51), p.32. The Constitution was amended again in 1985 and for details of changes see, O'Regan + O'Toole, (eds.) Green Book (1975-90) in New Irish Architecture, (No. 6, 1991), p.61.

viii Desmond FitzGerald, "Inaugural Address" in Green Book, (1948-49), p.27.

ix Ibid., p.28.

x Sam Stephenson, "Assessors' Comments" in New Irish Architecture, (No. 12, 1997), p.5.

xi FitzGerald, Green Book, (1948-9), p.24.

xii Ibid., "...a meeting place in which these interests can develop and grow will be of value. In throwing its membership open to the public, the Association is offering itself as such a forum. Starting slowly, no doubt, it may in time become a centre in which critics may air their views and, if necessary, expose the pretensions of work of which we, as architects, might be entirely unaware."

xiii Dermot O'Toole, "Inaugural Address" in Green Book, (1943-44) p.28 -9; J Morgan, "Inaugural Address" in Green Book, (1949-50), p.27.

xiv C Aliaga Kelly, "Inaugural Address" in Green Book, (1951-52) p.28.

xv Collins Shorter Dictionary and Thesaurus, (Harper Collins, 1991), p.175.

xvi Shane O'Toole, "Beautiful Pictures of Fine Buildings will not Change Public Perceptions. A Commentary on Ten Years of New Irish Architecture", in New Irish Architecture, (No.10, 1995), p.75.

xvii For a critical review of the first ten years of the award scheme, see Ibid., p.74-77. For an overview (i.e.: list and selected photographic representation) of the past twenty years of the NIA, see John O'Regan, "AAI Awards XX" in New Irish Architecture, (No.20, 2005), p.177-223.

xviii Since 1990 a non-architect has been invited to infiltrate the panel of judges. Assessors' comments, as they react to graphic and photographic representations of selected projects, can be read in the NIA publications.

xix John Mitchell (AAI President), "Introduction" in New Irish Architecture, (No.1, 1986), p.4.

xx Orna Hanly, (AAI President), "Introduction" in New Irish Architecture, (No.2, 1987).

xxi Shelley McNamara, "Assessors' Comments" in New Irish Architecture, (No. 14, 1999), p.6.

xxii The Irish Architectural Foundation was established in 2005. For more information see its recent festival website: www.lovingarchitecture.com Since 2000 Ireland has contributed at least one pavilion to the Venice Biennale: N3 by Tom de Paor (2000), Dooradoyle abstraction by Bucholz McEvoy (2002), Letterfrack Metamorph by O'Donnell Tuomey (2004). For more on O'Donnell Tuomey's highly acclaimed pavilion, see Transformation of an Institution. The Furniture College Letterfrack, (Gandon Editions, 2004).

xxiii As the third such consultant, the recently appointed, Emmet Scanlon, will "be responsible for providing policy advice to the Arts Council on architecture, and for developmental work in this artform." See press release on Wednesday 1st March 2006, www.artscouncil.ie/news

xxiv James O'Toole, "Inaugural Address" in Green Book, (1969-70) p.7.

xxv The National Library of Ireland seems to have the most complete set of Green Books although their annual publication does not follow the Association's history and activity. There are continuous breaks in its publication until the clear-run following the second World War until 1975. In between its publication and the New Irish Architecture the AAI issued the AAI News (Architectural Association of Ireland Newsletter. Other notable AAI publications during the latter half of the twentieth century include: Architectural Conservation: An Irish Viewpoint (A series of papers read to the AAI in 1973-74); Public Works: the Architecture of the Office of Public Works, 1831 – 1987, (ed by Ciaran O'Connor/John O'Regan, 1987); Building For Learning: Third-Level Educational Buildings in Ireland, (1986); finally the ongoing (since 1999) journal, Building Material.

xxvi Peter Ferguson, "In Dublin, for instance, we still do not have a City Architect. This is a disaster... Ireland has the worst record, after the UK, for holding architectural competitions. Sweden held 202 competitions in ten years, Finland about 120 and Denmark 120... our most successful buildings resulted from them – the Sugar Company, TCD library, the ESB and the UCD complex.", in "Inaugural Address 1971-72" in Green Book, (1971-75) p.12. Brian O'Connell, "Ireland has too often been the testing ground for imported systems and services... [and]... has had more than its fair share of foreign "experts" operating from outside this country... The attitude which favours the appointment of foreign advisers on public issues betrays an inferiority complex and at best is a waste of the professional resources which the country has developed.", in "Inaugural Address 1973-74" in Ibid., p.17.

xxvii For an example of this point see: Green Book, (1967-68) is dedicated to a discussion of urban form; Green Book, (1962) discusses rural architectural conservation and Modernist German church architecture; Green Book, (1964) "Sacred Architecture" by Richard Hurley p.30-33; Green Book, (1961) President's address concentrates on lost "Golden opportunity for Church building", Green Book, (1960) "Lecture Notes" on Church architecture by Fr Austin Flannery and so on...

xxviii Architectural Survey appears to be the most thorough record of Ireland's building in the 1950s and 1960s (and into the 1970s although I have only consulted one from this decade - 1972). Edited by Luan Cuffe from 1953-57 and then by Patrick Delaney from 1958-67. Both editors edited the Green Book following Sydney Maskell's resignation, and they both acted as AAI president. In this way then, the Architectural Survey could be read as the less 'intellectual' and more rooted in building counterpart of the AAI's publication. Building Survey, edited by Aodhagan Brioscu and partly in Irish, seems to take over as the annual record of building in Ireland from the late 1960s. From my knowledge of this publication, it is more politically motivated than Architectural Survey, the Green Book, or the RIAI Yearbook. The monthly journal PLAN is extremely interesting and polemical in the 1970s; it was edited by Uinseann MacEoin.

xxix Edward McParland, "Assessors' Comments" in New Irish Architecture, (No. 13, 1998), p.5.

xxx Joe Cleary, speaking at: "Revivals and Histories: Irish Criticism – its Past and Futures", 5th November 2005, Mater Dei Institute, Dublin 9.

xxxi Sean O Laoire, "Assessors' Comments" in New Irish Architecture, (No. 8, 1993), p.5.

xxxii C Aliaga Kelly, "Inaugural Address" in Green Book, (1951-52) p.25.

xxxiii Ibid., p.26.

xxxiv Sydney Maskell, "Inaugural Address 1949-50" in Green Book, (1949-50-51) p.25 and only eight pages on, in the same journal, Frank Purcell, "Inaugural Address 1940-51" in Ibid, p.33.

xxxv Competition brief, in Ibid., p.36-38. See also the hilarious brief for a house for Dr. Hawthorne Hastings: "The Doctor is not a man of habit, he generally rises at noon, but periodically throws the house into confusion by rising with the lark&Mrs Cosgar, married daughter, a widow with two children, boy and girl, four and five yrs old. She is a free lance journalist, living in England, but generally stays with her parents for about two out of twelve months. The length of her visits depend on the controversial temperature of the household, since she loves a dramatic exit almost as much as her father enjoys a sentimental reunion." Almost as an afterthought the brief outlines the spaces required, i.e.: Services, garage, yard, planting, site. And finally, there is a small amount of information on what must be submitted vis-à-vis drawings/word report/sketch plans etc. See Green Book, (1948-49) p.39-43.

xxxvi "Away with Leinster House (Study Group Report)", in Green Book, (1951-2), p.39.

xxxvii July 7 1964: "World Design" by Buckminster Fuller; April 20th 1965: "Work in Progress" by James Stirling, see Green Book, (1964 and 1965). For more on the content and significance of the AAI's lecture programme, see Part II of this review, (forthcoming issue of Building Material).

xxxviii Quoted by Desmond FitzGerald, "Inaugural Address" in Green Book, (1948-49), p.25.

xxxix Niall Montgomery "That'll All have to come down" in Green Book, (1956), p.81.

Frank Hall: An Obituary
SHELLEY MCNAMARA

I want to pay tribute to the architect Frank Hall.

We met around 1977..
I had never met anybody like him.
His passion for architecture knew no bounds.
His uncompromising search for truth and authenticity in work was merciless, confrontational.
His immersion in painting, literature, and politics was fired by a belief in Art and Humanity.
He was a distinct shock to the system.
When I met Frank I was, in my own work, tentative, hesitant, and dithering on the edge.
He had no patience for that. He told me that I suffered from 'academic rigor mortis'. He stated in no uncertain terms that Architecture was much bigger than all of us. All one had to do was to contribute in some small way to this great tradition. The type of encouragement he gave didn't feel like a gentle nudge or a push, more like a very severe kick over the edge. Jump in he said. Don't hold back. That was his way of thinking, living and working. He was a risk taker. Frank was my mentor.

He was a founder member of Grafton Architects.
We were a co-operative practice of five partners.
We thought about calling ourselves Cleary Farrell Hall McNamara & Murphy in alphabetical order. But this title was bulky and because of Frank's socio-political ideology, and the value he placed on the role of the individual within the collective we chose the more neutral title of Grafton Architects, favouring the group over the individual.
He had worked for three years in Seville, had subsequently been in private practice in Dublin and had completed a number of mews houses and houses on Adelaide Road.
We were two years out of college.
He made beautiful, assured, solid pencil drawings.
(A quality evident in Iseult's work many years later).
With Tony Murphy he collaborated on the detailing and construction of a brick house with a grass finished concrete vaulted roof, using the terracotta tiled ceiling as permanent shuttering... bravely executed with a small builder... a first for all involved.
The sense of measure, precision, materiality and building was evident in Frank's drawings. Although he was a risk taker, he anchored us in the task of building.

From our different training grounds there was a natural resonance and exchange between us.
He loved ideas but was ruthlessly practical.
He talked about the sensuality of materials. He talked about the 'smell' of architecture.
He broke into Spanish when our office got very hot in summer.
His work was lean, well edited, no inessentials;
'Err on the inessential side' he would say, quoting Kavanagh.

He was wary of 'design'. He abhorred preciousness.

He talked about democracy and architecture, how certai forms were democratic and other forms restrictive.
He talked about architecture being open to life, not exclusive, not prescriptive.
He was committed to the role of the architect in the provision of 'housing for the people', 'housing for the masses'.
(He later went on to practice with Shay Cleary for 6 years and together they completed a number of seminal housi projects in Harcourt Terrace, Swan Place and Chapelizod. his own right he completed numerous projects including apartment buildings in Portobello & Clanbrassil St.)

He was brilliant in the reading of a site, its potential, and its physical capacity.
He was brilliant at finding sites.
When he had no work he went out and found a site, foun a developer, put them together, and made a project
He loved quirky impossible sites which he could transform
He loved the city.

His view of commerce was a revelation. On certain occasions in those early heady days in Grafton Street, he suggested that fees should be divided according to the number of children one had. Frank had four, Tony had tw and Yvonne, Shay and I had none.
This commercial bent he later brought to bear on his ver productive career as developer/architect in collaboration with his great friend and partner Barry Meagher.

In these later years we also collaborated with Frank on a number of projects, where he was the architect/client or the architect /developer.
He was demanding but open and generous... Frank was always generous... and always demanding and sometim infuriating.
He would allow you to present your scheme and when y had finished he would take a piece of squared paper from his pocket with his own precise pencil plans, which wou be as inventive (or more so) than those which you had just presented to him.
He liked that!

Frank influenced and affected many architects of our generation. He was a catalyst. He was challenging. He made an important contribution to the architectural mili and culture in which he found himself.

Frank always talked about love. He loved you or he didn' love you. There was not much of an in-between with him He said you couldn't make architecture without love.
Love of life, love of radical thought, love of precision and clarity, love of the sensual, love of structure, of form, of spatial liberation, love of ideas, and love of humanity. I believed him then and I believe him now and I pay tribut to Architect Frank Hall.

Shelley McNamara is an architect and partner in Grafton Architects.
(As delivered at the funeral of Frank Hall on 20th May 2005 in Our Lad of Refuge Church, Rathmines)

AAI Membership Form

Dear Member, Associate Member, Honorary Member,
As a voluntary non-profit organisation our dependency on the support of our members is paramount. It is only through the continued involvement of our membership that the AAI can fulfil its charter 'to provide a medium of friendly communication between members and others interested in the progress of architecture'. To this end we look forward to seeing you at AAI events.

Regards,
The Committee

(PLEASE FILL OUT ALL IN BLOCK CAPITALS)

Membership term runs from 01/07/06 to 30/05/07

Name:

Address:

Email:

Nationality:

Membership category: ☐ (Please tick one from the list)

Student (school) _____ Year ☐

Important Notice Regarding Site Visits: The AAI Insurance Policy covers only paid-up members of the AAI, for instance children are NOT covered. Entrance to site would be refused to non-AAI members. It is also requested that AAI-members visiting sites provide their own safety equipment. Entrance to site could be refused for lack of safety equipment.

Membership category/fee structure

Full Membership

☐ **A**	Member (ordinary)	€80
☐ **B**	Member (retired or unemployed)	€20
☐ **C**	Member (student over 2nd Year)	€20
☐ **D**	Member (student 1st & 2nd Year)	Free
☐ **E**	Member (honorary)	Free

Associate member

☐ **F**	Associate member	€20
☐	(other than approved organisations*)	
☐ **G**	Associate Member (from 01/01 - 30/06)	€45
☐ **H**	Associate Member (from 01/04 - 30/06)	€30
J	Associate Member (single event - non student)	€10
K	Associate Member (single event - student)	€10

(*members of ICS, SSI and EEI)

Payment Details

Name:

Billing address:

Membership Category: _____ **(A-K)**

Applicable Fee:

Credit Card Payment

Visa ☐   Mastercard ☐   Other: ☐

Card Number:

Expiry date:

Signature: _____

Laser Card Payment (IN BLOCK)   BOI ☐   AIB ☐   OTHER ☐

Card Number:

Sort Code:

Expiry date:

Signature: _____

Phone No.

Office No.1, 43/44 Temple Bar, Dublin 2.
t: + 353 1 6351428 **f:** + 353 1 6351429
e: aaiadmin@eircom.net **w:** www.aai-architecture.ie

In the interest keeping our members up to date with all events, the AAI would like to encourage as many members that have the facility to recieve email to kindly fill out the folowing

☐ I would like to be reminded of AAI events by email
☐ I would like to recieve the AAI events by email (pdf format)

Age Group: 19-29 ☐   30-39 ☐   40-49 ☐   50-59 ☐   60+ ☐
AAI Lectures & Site visits qualify as 'Formal CPD activity' as approved by RIAI council

☐ Lectures   ☐ AAI Awards   ☐ Site Visits
☐ Exhibitions   ☐ Building Material   ☐ Social events (tennis tournament etc)

Lagan

PARTNERING AAI

Drumgil, Kingscourt, County Cavan

Tel: 042 966 7317 Fax: 042 966 7206

Email: info@kingscourtbricks.ie

Web:-   www.laganbrick.com